Gender and Violence in Haiti

Gender and Violence in Haiti

Women's Path from Victims to Agents

BENEDETTA FAEDI DURAMY

RUTGERS UNIVERSITY PRESS

NEW BRUNSWICK, NEW JERSEY, AND LONDON

Library of Congress Cataloging-in-Publication Data
Faedi Duramy, Benedetta.
Gender and violence in Haiti : women's path from victims to agents / Benedetta Faedi Duramy.
    pages cm
Includes bibliographical references and index.
ISBN 978-0-8135-6315-2 (hardcover : alk. paper) — ISBN 978-0-8135-6314-5
(pbk. : alk. paper) — ISBN 978-0-8135-6316-9 (e-book)
    1. Women—Violence against—Haiti. 2. Girls—Violence against—Haiti. 3. Sex
crimes—Zimbabwe—Mbare. 4. Abused women—Haiti. 5. Family violence—Haiti.
6. Female offenders—Haiti. 7. Women—Legal status, laws, etc.—Haiti. I. Title.
HV6250.4.W65F34 2014
362.88082'097294—dc23   2013029875

A British Cataloging-in-Publication record for this book is available from
the British Library.

Visit our website: http://rutgerspress.rutgers.edu

Manufactured in the United States of America

For Johan, the love of my life, and our little Leonardo

CONTENTS

ACKNOWLEDGMENTS

This book could have not been either started or successfully completed without the support and contributions of several people to whom I am therefore profoundly grateful. My deepest gratitude goes to Deborah Rhode, whose encouragement, remarkable expertise in gender discrimination, and genuine devotion to women's rights have been an incommensurable source of inspiration and example. For support and thoughtful comments, I am also thankful to Jenny S. Martinez, Helen Stacy, Lawrence Freedman, Manuel Gomez, Deborah Hensler, Allen Weiner, Terry Karl, Amalia Kessler, Richard Roberts, George Letsas, Monica McDermott, Michelle Mckinley, Allegra McLeod, Michael Musheno, Mary Ellen O'Connell, Sarah Paoletti, Nadine Puechguirbal, Natalie Man, Carol Shabrami, Sofia Candeias, Barron Bixler, Allison Carruth, Dara Kay Cohen, and Matteo Lodevole. I also thank my editor, Marlie Wassernman, at Rutgers University Press, for her precious suggestions and, more important, for believing in this book.

This study could have not been possible without the generous support of the following institutions: Golden Gate University School of Law, a group of faculty colleagues and the library staff; Stanford Law School, the Freeman Spogli Institute for International Studies at Stanford University, the Michelle Clayman Institute for Gender Research at Stanford University, the Stanford Center on International Conflict and Negotiation, the Stanford Office of the Vice Provost for Graduate Education, the Gerald J. Lieberman Fellowship Fund at Stanford University; and, finally, the Arthur C. Helton Fellowship Program of the American Society of International Law.

At a practical and emotional level, I am very thankful to the following people. My parents, whose intellectual integrity and respect for the ultimate meaning of service and justice are fixed in my memory, lead my ordinary actions, and emboldened me, in spite of any other consideration, to pursue my heartfelt dreams. My husband, Johan, who brightens up each of my days and shares with steadfast love our everyday life as well as hope and promises for the future; and, finally, our son, Leonardo, who joined us at the late stage of my writing and patiently napped or played next to me while I was completing this book. I wish for him a better world and even more happiness and adventures than the ones I have been so fortunate to enjoy.

I owe immense recognition to the everyday efforts of those Haitian women and victims who fight in many different ways for countering gender-based violence and reclaiming equality and protection for their daughters and themselves. To them and all the other participants in this study, who unstintingly work to make even the smallest contribution to changing this world into a more just place, go my full consideration and immense gratitude. Finally, my thoughts go to the memory of all friends and informants of this book who died in the earthquake that affected Haiti on January 12, 2010.

"Que la terre vous soit légère."

ACRONYMS AND ORGANIZATIONS

AFASDA. Association Femmes Soleil d'Haiti; civil society organization

AVSI. Association of Volunteers in International Service; international NGO

CEDAW. Convention on the Elimination of All Forms of Discrimination against Women

CHREPROF. Centre Haïtien de Recherches et d'Actions pour la Promotion Féminine

DDR programs. disarmament, demobilization, and reintegration programs

ENFOFANM. Organization for the Defense of Women's Rights

GHESKIO. Le Groupe Haïtien d'Etude du Sarcome de Kaposi et des Infections Opportunistes/Haitian Group for the Study of Kaposi's Sarcoma and Opportunistic Infections; national NGO

IBERS. Institut du Bien-Etre Social et de la Recherche/Institute of Social Well-Being and Research

ICRC. International Committee of the Red Cross

IFES. International Foundation for Electoral Systems

IOM. International Organization for Migration

IRB. Institutional Review Board

Kay Fanm. civil society organization

KOFAVIV. Komisyon Fanm Viktim pou Viktim/Commission of Women Victims for Victims; civil society organization

Kopadim. civil society organization

MDM. Médecins du Monde

MINUSTAH. United Nations Stabilization Mission in Haiti

Mouvement des Femmes Haitiennes. Haitian Women's Movement

MSF. Médecins sans Frontières/Doctors without Borders

NGO. non-governmental organization

OAS. Organization of American States

OZANFAN. Organizasyon Zanmi Fanmi; civil society organization

Padre Stra. religious organization

PNH. Haitian National Police

SOFA. Solidarity Fanm Ayisyen; civil society organization

Suor Anna. religious organization

Tribunal des Mineurs. Tribunal for Minors

UNDP. United Nations Development Programme

UNFPA. United Nations Population Fund

UNICEF. United Nations International Children's Emergency Fund

UNIFEM. United Nations Development Fund for Women

UNPOL. United Nations Police Department

UNSMIH. United Nations Support Mission in Haiti

URAMEL. Unité de Recherche et de Action Médico Légale

Viva Rio. international NGO

WFP. World Food Program

WHO. World Health Organization

Gender and Violence in Haiti

Introduction

Current scholarship as well as international policy studies focusing on civil conflicts and armed violence have construed women as victims and men as perpetrators of violence. This prevalent interpretation tells part of the story, but it leaves out an equally important dimension: women as participants in violence and men occasionally as victims. This book joins the emerging effort to highlight limitations in the conventional wisdom and to enlarge understandings of why women engage in violence. To that end, this study focuses in particular on women and girls in the slum communities of Haiti. It explores the nexus between their prior victimization by sexual abuse and their subsequent decision to join armed factions. This research is informed by other studies addressing the relationship between violence against women and women's participation in violence in several countries torn apart by civil or military conflicts. This book, however, provides the first empirical analysis of Haiti's high prevalence of sexual violence and female involvement in armed violence.

Specifically, this study aims at shedding light on girls' and women's internalization of gender stereotypes and their experience of violence, which engenders common patterns of retaliation. It investigates the incentives, conditions, and decision-making processes that motivate victims of rape and sexual abuse to join armed groups and to become actively affiliated with and perpetrators of violence. By investigating the current international legal norms for and Haitian legislation on both female victimization and female aggression, this analysis aims at contributing to the design of effective measures to free women from violence, to dispel their anger and resentment toward ineffective forms of community reconciliation, and to improve their reintegration into society.

This empirical research has been informed by longitudinal fieldwork conducted during a total of twelve months between June 2006 and December 2008 in the three cities of Haiti that are primarily affected by armed violence—Port-au-Prince, Cap-Haitien, and Gonaives. The research design included in-depth face-to-face interviews, focus groups, and participant observation. It involved a heterogeneous sample of informants comprised of women who either had been victims of violence or had been members of armed groups, in addition to representatives of international and national institutions or civil society organizations working on the issues of women and armed violence in the country.

Pursuing this research in Haiti, in the midst of political uncertainty, social discontent, violent confrontations, and brutal reprisals against the resident population and foreigners, has been a challenging, but insightful, experience. Every work is partially the fruit of personal events that capture one's attention and create incentives and memories, and so is this. Two very different episodes, in which I was either a powerless spectator or a silent and compassionate listener, motivated me to contemplate the unfortunate and hostile destiny of Haitian women and girls.

During my stay in Port-au-Prince during one of my fieldtrips, I was driven home one night by UN personnel as a security measure. I glimpsed an unusual and eerie movement on my side of the street. Drawing nearer to the window, in the darkness of a secondary narrow path that was rugged and almost entirely obstructed by garbage, I saw a group of young men forcibly dragging a little girl and beating her on the head while she struggled. I jumped up in my seat and screamed to stop the car, but safety rules require personnel on such occasions to leave the area and promptly report the case by radio to security forces. We did, but when the patrol arrived at the place, only a few minutes later, they could not find any trace of the victim or her assailants. I will never know what happened, but I thought about that night and the little girl for a long time.

Only a few days later, through an informant from Médecins sans Frontières/Doctors without Borders (MSF), I arranged an interview with two representatives—victims themselves—of a national organization providing primary medical assistance to girls affected by sexual violence in a conflict area of Port-au-Prince. Because, according to security measures, I was not authorized to enter the area, both women consented to travel for one and half hours each way, in the midst of political demonstrations and disorder, to reach the United Nations International Children's Emergency Fund (UNICEF) compound where I was temporarily staying. On the day the meeting was scheduled, I waited for them in vain. Later I learned that they had come, but the receptionist, suspicious of their intentions, had sent them away. Nevertheless, both women agreed to return the following day, not for money but for the sole purpose of telling their stories. After a long, stressful, and poignant interview, they anxiously asked me to keep their names and participation confidential, fearing possible retaliation against their families or themselves. For security reasons, their identities, like those of all other informants for this study, remain hidden, but the narratives from all these sources have inspired this book.

Research Sites

The fieldwork for this research study was conducted in the three major urban settings of Haiti primarily affected by armed violence—Port-au-Prince, Cap-Haitien, and Gonaives. I deliberately selected these research sites in order to assess variations, if any, in the levels of sexual violence experienced by girls and women as well as in their active participation in armed violence. In the end, most of the data were collected in Port-au-Prince, the capital of the country, because of the centralization there of Haitian institutions and the concentration of non-governmental organizations (NGOs), civil society organizations, and international agencies.

Located in the central western part of the country on the Gulf of Gonaives, Port-au-Prince is the principal seaport and commercial center of Haiti. Because of poor and unregulated urban planning, the city is sprawling and is almost 800 percent more densely populated than London. According to a study conducted in the early 1990s, a full two-thirds of Haitians residing in the capital were migrants (Manigat 1997). The great exodus from the countryside began in the mid-1980s, when a crisis in the agricultural economy forced many farmers to relocate to the city in search of manufacturing jobs (Kovats-Bernat 2006, 24).

Once covered with rich soil and luxuriant vegetation, Haiti's forests have increasingly disappeared over the last two centuries. Nowadays, the trees cover less than 5 percent of the country, less than 20 percent of its soil is cultivable, and only 3 percent of that soil is irrigated (Kovats-Bernat 2006, 25). Stressed by unbearable poverty for decades, hungry farmers have ignorantly deforested their land to plant fast-growing but soil-impoverishing crops, to build houses, or to produce charcoal. The depletion of land, lack of arable soil, and proliferation of factories encouraged mass emigration of rural inhabitants to Port-au-Prince.

The provincial exodus has not dwindled over the last few decades. According to the World Bank, over thirteen thousand rural migrants pour into the capital every year. Such massive migration has caused overpopulation as well as the deterioration of urban space, security, and basic services for the inhabitants. Prolonged state neglect and mismanagement have caused "the entire city of Port-au-Prince [to acquire] the physiognomy of a slum. . . . Entire neighborhoods are constructed in a course of a month, as the pace of family-organized construction of makeshift dwellings accelerates. In no time at all, spaces where before construction was prohibited or that were scarcely populated are covered by networks of houses completely lacking in basic services. . . . The marginalized people hurl themselves at the task of conquering any chink of available terrain. The city is the contested terrain of this struggle" (Manigat 1997, 90). As a result, Port-au-Prince has expanded into numerous districts and many low-income shantytowns that are plagued with poverty and violence.

Probably the most notorious and dangerous slum of the capital is Cité Soleil, situated at the northern edge of the city, at the base of overshadowing mountains, adjacent to the sea and the airport. The congested streets of Cité Soleil taper off into dirty alleys surrounded by high concrete walls; the alleys are crowded with pigs, garbage, and houses constructed from cardboard, plaster, and tin. In the midst of misery, disarray, and violence, streets often become *salon pèp*, the people's living room.[1] "They become places for work, places to socialize, and for some, places to sleep, eat, and live. In Haiti to be sure, the street is for most an end in itself" (Kovats-Bernat 2006, 31).

The first and perhaps only ethnographic map ever made of Cité Soleil, dated 1992, divided the community into six areas: Brooklyn, Linthau,

Drouillard, Parc Industriel, Boston, and Centre (Bernard et al. 1993). These areas are then further split into small neighborhoods with little greenery, open sewers, and numerous hot and dumpy shacks. Indeed, "no one really wants to live in Cité Soleil. It is noisy, dirty, politically turbulent, and violent, but it offers cheap housing, the cheapest in all of the capital" (Maternowska 2006, 3). During the rainy season, most of the paths become muddy streams and puddles smelling of rotten garbage. In 2008, a series of violent storms flooded Cité Soleil, dragging huts and valuables away.

Some areas of the slum still do not have electricity. A representative of MSF once told me that, after sunset, young students crouch under the windows of the Cité Soleil hospital looking for light to finish their homework. Only a few primary and secondary schools are functioning in Cité Soleil. Sometimes, they are too far away for children who cannot afford to ride in *tap taps* (gaily painted buses or pick-up trucks that serve as share taxis), the most common form of mass transportation in Haiti. For girls, crossing different districts to reach the school can also be dangerous. They might end up trapped in armed confrontations between rival gangs and become victims of sexual violence as a means of retaliation. School fees for tuition, books, and uniforms are usually too expensive for most families living in Cité Soleil. Only a few nonprofit organizations provide primary education for children and professional training in home economics and crafts for teenagers.

For security reasons, the majority of civil society organizations working on gender-based violence and women's violence are not based in Cité Soleil or the other conflict zones of Port-au-Prince. During an interview, representatives of Komisyon Fanm Viktim pou Viktim/Commission of Women Victims for Victims (KOFAVIV), an organization run by and for victims of sexual violence, reported that they had been forced under threat to move their office, originally located in Martissant, to a safer area of the city. Other civil society organizations operating in Port-au-Prince include Kay Fanm and Solidarity Fanm Ayisyen (SOFA), both of which provide psychological and legal assistance to victims, and Le Groupe Haïtien d'Etude du Sarcome de Kaposi et des Infections Opportunistes/Haitian Group for the Study of Kaposi's Sarcoma and Opportunistic Infections (GHESKIO), which specializes in providing medical assistance as well as psychological support.

The slums in Gonaives and Cap-Haitien look very similar to those in Cité Soleil, and they are equally plagued by misery and violence. Situated in northern Haiti, Gonaives is the capital of the Artibonite Department. It is also known as Haiti's City of Independence because it was there on the Place d'Armes that, in 1804, Jean Jacque Dessalines proclaimed the island independent from France. In the early 2000s, Gonaives became the scene of armed confrontations between the supporters of President Jean Bertrand Aristide's government and the opposition group Revolutionary Artibonite Resistance Front. In 2004, the Revolutionary Artibonite Resistance Front took control of the city, starting the rebellion that in the end overturned Aristide's government. In 2004 and in 2008, Gonaives was devastated by catastrophic hurricanes that killed hundreds of people and left thousands homeless.

Cap-Haitien is a city of about 190,000 inhabitants situated on the north cost of Haiti. It was an important town during the colonial period and the original capital of the country after its independence from France. Historically, Cap-Haitien has been an incubator for revolutionary movements and antigovernment factions. In 2004, the city was taken over by the military junta that overturned Aristide and forced him into exile. The central area of the city is surrounded on the east side by the Bay of Cap-Haitien and on the west by mountains, which are increasingly dominated by flimsy urban slums. Very few civil society organizations working on gender-based violence and women's violence are based in Gonaives or Cap-Haitien. SOFA has small local units in both cities and the nearby countryside. In addition, specific programs sponsored by the United Nations or UNICEF have operated in these areas with the cooperation of the Ministry for the Status of Women.

Notes from the Field

The data and observations for this study draw on twelve months of fieldwork spread across six trips to Haiti between July 2006 and December 2008. I first visited Haiti in 2006, when I worked as a researcher for the Child Protection Unit of the United Nations Stabilization Mission in Haiti (MINUSTAH) in Port-au-Prince for two months. At that time, I primarily contributed to the preparation of the input document on Haiti for the report of the Secretary-General on children and armed conflict for the UN Security Council (United Nations General Assembly/Security Council 2006). In particular, I was responsible for monitoring, gathering information on, and drafting legal opinions on the widespread and systematic perpetration of rape and sexual abuse against girls in the country. During this visit, I had the opportunity to engage in preliminary research as well as to attend seminars and institutional workshops on sexual violence.

Given the outbreak of violence in the politically turbulent communities of Port-au-Prince and the subsequent and continual status of alert and insecurity for international people in the rest of the city, the curfews imposed by MINUSTAH at that point provided a certain degree of protection for its personnel and affiliates. Although these security measures, on the one hand, significantly constrained my movements and access to victims, potential informants, and settings of violations, on the other hand, they eventually were my only form of protection.

Despite my initial collaboration with the Child Protection Unit of MINUSTAH, the empirical research informing this book was not conducted under the auspices of MINUSTAH or in conjunction with any UN study or assessment. Indeed, the independence of my study was crucial to building trustful relationships with my informants, especially with victims and women involved with armed groups as well as with representatives of civil society organizations, who are sometimes critical of MINUSTAH's position and influence in the Haitian community. Unconnected to this empirical study, my occasional collaboration with the Child Protection Unit to provide insights on gender-based violence and adequate strategies to address it has indeed benefited from my understanding of such issues. However, the fact that I also operated with the international community and organizations helped me to understand their role in the Haitian context and sometimes to channel their resources to support programs and initiatives designed by local organizations.

When I returned to Port-au-Prince in December 2006, the situation of the country had degenerated tremendously. Despite the attempt of President René García Préval to pursue a conciliatory tack with opposing armed groups, gang leaders resisted surrendering their armies, refused to negotiate with the government, and continued wreaking havoc on the country. At the end of the year, rapes, killings, and especially kidnappings of foreigners, national officers of international organizations, and even school buses filled with children erupted throughout Port-au-Prince and forced the government to hasten MINUSTAH military operations in the slums.

In this setting data collection became a difficult and complicated process. Because access to deprived communities was extremely dangerous, I organized most of my meetings with informants in MINUSTAH and other international institutions' offices, the Ministry for the Status of Women, the Hotel Montana, and public places within the authorized areas of the city. At that time traveling throughout the country was equally dangerous, so I had to cancel my initial plan to include informants in Gonaives and Cap-Haitien.

In my subsequent field trips to Haiti, I developed a strong connection with some of the victims and women engaged in violence whom I interviewed multiple times. I admired their courage and their willingness to help other women by establishing civil society organizations or simply by organizing support groups. In other victims, I perceived a sadness that I had never seen before or an anger that could never be assuaged. By spending entire days with them in focus groups or in one-on-one interviews, I often felt somehow responsible for them and compelled to provide assistance.

During the summer of 2007, I heard from a friend working for MINUSTAH that funds were available for projects related to women and children affected by armed violence. Although I knew that the women running a particular civil society organization with which I was familiar were completely unprepared to deal with the administration and requirements of the United Nations, I recommended them as one of the best organizations in Haiti working for the rehabilitation of victims of violence. After a long and elaborate process, the section of MINUSTAH that is responsible for the disarmament, demobilization, and reintegration (DDR) of Haitians either affected or involved in armed violence finally decided to support one of their projects designed to provide education to children affected by armed violence.

MINUSTAH agreed to support the organization, provided that a competent coordinator was responsible for the budget and for monitoring and reporting on the project. The women in charge of the organization asked me to help them, offering me the leading role. I faced then the difficult choice of pursuing my research or becoming an active participant in their cause. With some reluctance, I declined their offer. However, together with MINUSTAH representatives I helped them to select a suitable candidate for the job. Since then, the MINUSTAH DDR Unit has agreed to continue funding this project, thus supporting the education of hundreds of Haitian children who have been victims of violence.

In December 2007, another escalation of kidnapping in Port-au-Prince targeted bourgeois Haitian families and international residents. The teenage son of one of my acquaintances was kidnapped with a friend, late at night, as they were coming out of a club and were on their way home. Although his family promptly paid the ransom requested, awaiting the son's release became a long agony. Only a few days later, a married couple working for the European Union was kidnapped upon leaving the house of some friends. The man was almost immediately released after the payment of the ransom. His wife, however, was kept in custody for over a week, was brutally assaulted, and was finally abandoned in shock in the middle of a slum.

These two events, combined with the intensity of my interviews with victims as well as the women implicated in armed violence, reignited my fear for my own safety. Whenever I was driving, I started carefully check-ing whether the cars behind were following me; I changed the routes and times of my ride every day. At night, after a long day of work, focus-group sessions, and interviews, I began to visualize some of my informants' sto-ries and had trouble falling asleep. I also developed groundless and irratio-nal worries for my family in Europe or faraway dear friends. At the end of my stay, I flew back to the United States feeling that a good break was much needed and appropriate.

I returned to Haiti in June 2008 to conduct fieldwork for the entire summer. At that time, I often visited Gonaives and Cap-Haitien to collect data and meet with informants. In September 2008, a violent hurricane followed by a series of storms devastated the country. Sadly, I saw first-hand the aftermath of flooding in Gonaives. Large portions of the city were covered in more than 1,800,000 cubic meters of mud. MINUSTAH esti-mated that 250,000 persons were affected, including a death toll of 466 in the floods and 235 missing (United Nations Security Council 2009). Some children were crying and running around barefoot in search of their parents. Others were playing with the remains of the devastation. Although Port-au-Prince was less affected by the storms, for me the heavy rains pouring down the streets like waterfalls and the hot wind that suddenly moved the clouds to obscure the sky were frightening. Some of the poor Haitians I knew lost family members and homes in the city of Jacmel, situated on the southeast coast of the country. My final visit to Haiti was in December 2008. I went back one last time to complete my fieldwork and to verify some of the data collected during my previous stays.

Research Methods

This research study used a qualitative-research design to gauge the meaning women ascribed to their experiences with violence as well as the incentives and decision-making processes that motivated them to retaliate. The sample of informants included rape victims, some of whom may also have been involved with gangs, and representatives of international and national institutions and civil society organizations dealing with violence. The study draws on 150 in-depth interviews and ten focus-group sessions with victims living in the slum communities of Port-au-Prince, Gonaives, and Cap-Haitien. It also draws on observations of support groups for victims at the shelters of civil society organizations.

Considering the sensitive nature of the issue under investigation and the lack of aggregate data, a nonrandom-sampling methodology was necessary. Records of cases and victims of sexual assaults are kept only sporadically by organizations of Haitian civil society, and to date no national aggregate data on these issues are available. Thus, a random-sampling methodology was impossible.

Given the difficulties in gaining access to women and girls involved in violence, the best method of identifying participants was through personal contacts within international and national institutions. To identify victims, civil society organizations providing medical and psychological assistance to rape victims, some of whom were also actively involved in community violence, drew on their extensive records of patients to arrange my encounters with those who, in their opinion, could easily handle the interviews according to their own recovery processes.

To gain a broad perspective on women's motives for participating in violence, as well as on effective legal proposals and policy recommendations, I interviewed a diverse sample of informants: rape victims living in the slums of Port-au-Prince, Gonaives, and Cap-Haitien; women and girls affected by armed violence who decided, at some stage in their lives, to join gangs and become perpetrators of violence; and women and girls in custody in the female prison at Port-au-Prince who were accused of the offense of association with armed groups.

My sample of informants who were related to international organizations and nongovernmental organizations (NGOs) included professional civilian personnel of MINUSTAH working in the field of violence against women and women's violence within the following offices: Child Protection Unit; Gender Unit; Human Rights Section; Special Investigation Unit of the Human Rights Section; Code of Conduct Unit; and the DDR Unit; the United Nations Police Department (UNPOL) and its Justice and Correction Unit; professional officers of UNICEF in Haiti, who are responsible for programs related to violence against and abuse of children as well as of children in conflict with the law; professional officers of both the United Nations Development Fund for Women (UNIFEM) and the United Nations Population Fund (UNFPA) in Haiti, who are responsible for programs related to violence against women, women's reintegration into society, and gender equality and empowerment; representatives of the International Organization for Migration (IOM) in Port-au-Prince, which funds programs for children in domestic service, some of whom have been sexually abused; representatives of the official delegation of the Inter-American Commission on Human Rights, who were conducting a visit to Haiti in December 2006 in regard to violence against women in the country and victims' access to justice and medical services; and representatives of international NGOs working in the conflict areas of Port-au-Prince in the field of sexual violations against women and armed violence, such as MSF, Médecins du Monde, Save the Children, the International Committee of the Red Cross (ICRC), Plan International Haiti, Association of Volunteers in International Service (AVSI), and Viva Rio (an NGO promoting peace and social development through direct programming and research).

At national institutions, I interviewed representatives of the Ministry of Justice based in Port-au-Prince; representatives of the Ministry for the Status of Women based in Port-au-Prince, Gonaives, and Cap-Haitien; representatives of the Ministry of Social Affairs based in Gonaives and Cap-Haitien; representatives of the Institut du Bien-Etre Social et de la Recherche/the Institute of Social Well-Being and Research (IBERS)—who are based in Port-au-Prince, Gonaives, and Cap-Haitien; prosecutors and magistrates working for the general Tribunal and the Tribunal des Mineurs/Tribunal for Minors; police officers of the Haitian National Police (PNH) and its division dealing with minors, the Brigade de Protection des Mineurs; the director of the female prison in Port-au-Prince; the members of the Bar Council's legal board in Port-au-Prince; and the representative of the Ombudsman Haiti.[2]

Finally, I interviewed representatives of national NGOs and institutions working in the conflict areas of Port-au-Prince in the field of violence against women and women's violence including Unité de Recherche et de Action Médico Légale (URAMEL), GHESKIO, International Foundation for Electoral Systems (IFES), SOFA, Kay Fanm, Organization for the Defense of Women's Rights (ENFOFANM), KOFAVIV, and Kopadim (a civil society organization providing education, support, and loans to victims of sexual violence and their children); representatives of Association Femmes Soleil d'Haiti (AFASDA), a civil society organization based in Gonaives that works on gender-based violence and women's violence; representatives of Organizasyon Zanmi Fanmi (OZANFAN), a civil society organization based in Cap-Haitien dealing with violence against women and their participation in armed violence; the parish priest of the Catholic church in Martissant, who is the director of a specific program for *restavèks;*[3] other religious organizations, including Padre Stra and Suor Anna, that provide shelters and both school and vocational education to rape victims and women involved in armed violence; professors of psychology at the University of Port-au-Prince whose work focuses on gender-based violence and prostitution in Haiti; and a professor of sociology at the University of Port-au-Prince who studies rape in Haiti.

Because conducting interviews with victims of rape and women involved in armed violence is a sensitive and emotionally wrenching task for the interviewee as well as for the interviewer and requires enough time to build a trusting relationship between the two, only those victims who spontaneously volunteered to share their experience with violence were included as participants in this study. Interviewees as well as women attending the focus groups or the support groups were given information about the project to ascertain whether they still wanted to participate. Informed consent was obtained from all the participants according to the Institutional Review Board (IRB) ethical rules.

Although the sample size for this study was relatively big, the findings of the investigation are not representative of the entire female population in Haiti. Nevertheless, the variety of the informants as well as their specific knowledge and experience in the field may compensate for the potential limitations of the initial outcomes. Moreover, because the goals of the research were to gain insight into the motivations that rape victims have to join armed groups and to formulate recommendations for reform, the essence of the project does not depend on having a statistically representative sample. The findings are not intended to convey all the opinions and approaches of institutional actors, the totality of victims' experiences and perceptions, or the frequency of particular motivations. Rather the purpose is to display cultural patterns of violence experienced or committed by women in order to inform potential future strategies and practical intervention measures.

The interviews included open-ended questions to accommodate extended narratives and to evoke personal memories and opinions as well as to comprehend decision-making processes and local understanding. I conducted the interviews in English, French, or Haitian Creole; they were scheduled from thirty minutes to two hours. The interviews with victims, in particular, focused on personal information, patterns of abuse and sexual violence, and involvement with armed groups, if any. The discussions covered their memories and their understanding of incentives, responsibility, and decision-making processes.

The interviews with representatives of international and national institutions and civil society organizations elicited representative instances of violence—either experienced or committed by girls and women—that were the objectives of their work. The discussions covered potential explanations for the widespread and systematic sexual violence affecting girls and women in Haiti as well as for the motives for joining armed groups. Furthermore, the informants were invited to describe existing approaches and programs adopted by their organizations or institutions aimed at protecting women from violence or addressing women's violence. All participants were also asked about potential strategies and practical measures that should be implemented to address the research topic and to improve their work in this field.

Focus-group sessions sought to facilitate the sharing of information and experiences among some of the informants and to elicit common themes and varied responses. Each focus group included about seven women from the same neighborhood who had been victims of sexual violence or who may have been involved with gangs at some point in their lives or both. Focus-group sessions took place in a quiet, private room on the premises of the shelter that provides primary medical and psychological assistance to rape victims. Discussions were conducted in either French or Haitian Creole and lasted about two hours each. A translator and a psychologist for the organization attended the meetings as well.

In order to corroborate my data, interpret victims' behaviors, and contextualize their stories, I also participated as an observer in support-group sessions designed for rape victims by national civil society organizations within their psychological-recovery programs. Support groups were held four days per week on the premises of the safe haven and were conducted by specialized personnel working for the organization. During the sessions, I took field notes and wrote reflections on the activities of the participants as well as noting their interaction, debates, and antagonistic or conciliatory attitudes.

The data gathered from interview/focus-group transcripts and field notes were thematically coded to assess common patterns of sexual harm, emotional distress, and rationale for retaliation. Pseudonyms were used to ensure protection and the privacy of participants' identities and organizations. Finally, in order to corroborate the findings obtained by the qualitative-research methods adopted in this study as well as to examine concepts and to substantiate the analysis of the pertinence of the findings, I reviewed international law, historical information and information from the social sciences as well as prior research studies, official reports, public documents, and media coverage on the research topic.

The remainder of this book is organized as follows. Chapter 1 presents the historical and social context for violence against women and female violence in Haiti. Slavery, a warlike past, economic deprivation, and political instability have laid foundations for gender-based violence. They are essential factors within the greater context in which human-rights violations occur as well as important tools for the development of this book. This chapter introduces the themes of the book by mapping the conditions for widespread gender-based violence and women's motivations for participating in armed groups.

Chapter 2 explores Haitian cultural beliefs concerning gender, which underpin private and public practices of sexual violence and exploitation. Unbalanced power relationships and domestic abuse diminish girls' and women's status within Haitian social hierarchies and ultimately generate patterns of gender-based violence that become weapons of war. Widely employed as a tool of terror and oppression, rape against women is deeply embedded in Haitian society; it shapes gender relationships in both private and public spheres. The chapter examines the correlations between gender discrimination and sexual abuse in the private realm and gender-based violence in the public domain.

Chapter 3 reviews the current literature on female participation in conflict and armed violence. It also examines the conditions and rationales that motivate women to become involved with armed groups. In-depth interviews, participant observation, and focus-group discussions show that the three major factors that motivate women and girls to engage in criminal and community violence are their need to protect themselves and their families, their resentment toward state negligence and denial of their plight, and their dysfunctional desire to attain personal and social respect through retaliation.

Chapter 4 describes the main international legal norms—international human-rights and humanitarian law—protecting women and girls from sexual violence in conflict settings as well as addressing their involvement in violence. It also examines the Haitian legal regime designed for the protection of victims of sexual violence and the prosecution of girls and women associated with gangs. The focus is on ways that national compliance with international obligations can affect gender-based violence and female participation in armed violence.

Chapter 5 investigates rape victims' reluctance to seek help and to report sexual assaults to relevant authorities. By examining women's decision making and resistance to state interventions, the analysis reveals the inadequacies of the Haitian law-enforcement and judicial systems. The underreporting of women's rights violations, the loss of rape cases at various stages of the criminal-justice process, and, ultimately, the widespread impunity enjoyed by those who perpetrate sexual violence derive from the victims' internalization of gender stereotypes and hierarchy, their fear of social stigmatization and reprisal, and the significant corruption, dysfunction, and gender bias within the security and judicial sectors.

Chapter 6 assesses the specific programs designed by international and civil society organizations that are aimed at reintegrating rape victims and female participants of armed and community violence into Haitian society. The analysis ultimately suggests strategies for action, including preventive, legal, and policy measures. Taken together such recommendations constitute an agenda for increasing both the protection of women and girls and their active participation in community reconciliation.

Finally, Chapter 7 recounts the devastation of the 2010 Haitian earthquake and the further violence that displaced women and children have been suffering from because of their increasing economic and physical vulnerability. International reporters working in the country have documented that, in the midst of desperation and disarray, women and girls have been daily victims of rape in the makeshift camps for the displaced. This chapter provides accounts of the different risks and patterns of violence affecting women and girls after the earthquake. It also suggests practical measures for tackling the current situation, and it reemphasizes that the ultimate eradication of gender-based violence and female violence can be achieved only by understanding their interplay in women's decision making and by implementing long-term strategies for interventions, as discussed in the previous chapters of this book.

On January 12, 2010, a 7.0-magnitude earthquake devastated the Haitian capital of Port-au-Prince and much of the surrounding countryside. Hundreds of thousands of Haitians lost their lives and about three million people—one-third of Haiti's population—were affected by the quake. Schools, hospitals, houses, offices, shops, the presidential palace, the cathedral, and the headquarters of the UN mission collapsed. Among the many who lost their lives in the tragedy, both Haitians and foreigners, were some of my close friends as well as participants in this study. Public attention has been necessarily focusing on rebuilding efforts and meeting basic needs. However, given the increasing economic and physical vulnerability of displaced women and girls, identifying effective responses to the root causes of gender-based violence and women's retaliation are now more urgent than ever.

By offering an engaged empirical analysis of the practices of violence against women and their motivations to retaliate prior to the earthquake as well as an examination of such patterns of violence after the natural disaster, this book tells a full story of Haitian women's experience with violence, both as victims and as perpetrators. It also serves the compelling purpose of guiding international aid and humanitarian organizations toward funding adequate programs and interventions to protect women and girls in Haiti from gender-based violence and recruitment by armed groups as well as of ensuring their active participation in the rebuilding efforts.

1

Gender-Based Violence and Women's Violence in Context

The Republic of Haiti is located in the Caribbean between Cuba and Puerto Rico and shares the island of Hispaniola with the Dominican Republic. Separated from the Florida coast of the United States by only one hour by air, Haiti has a unique historical heritage. No proper analysis of gender-based violence and women's violence in the country is possible without an understanding of its traumatic history. Slavery, a warlike past, and poverty are important lenses through which to appreciate the root cultural causes of the current practices of violence, which taint the power balance between men and women and impair the status of women within Haitian social hierarchies. This chapter presents these historical roots of gender discrimination and sexual abuse in Haiti, tracing the relationship between political and economic violence, which ultimately led to the current widespread insecurity of women and their everyday struggles with survival and protection.

From Slavery to Independence

Originally inhabited by the peaceful native population of Arawak, who called their land Haiti (mountainous land), the island was discovered by Christopher Columbus in 1492. Renamed Hispaniola (Spanish island), it became the first Spanish settlement in the New World. Over the first 150 years of its colonization, the Spanish focused primarily on the eastern part of the region, which appeared to be more prosperous in resources. Disease, massive killing, and enslavement by the Europeans fostered the progressive disappearance of the Arawak and ultimately led to their extinction. Because the Spanish had introduced the cultivation of sugar cane to the region and needed forced labor for the cane fields, they turned to the slave trade and imported thousands of African slaves to the island.

Attracted by the conspicuous resources of the Caribbean lands and the potential income, the French took advantage of Spain's lack of attention and began to occupy the western half of Hispaniola in 1659. Expanding their influence and claiming their own rights within the region, the French finally obtained official control of the western part of the island in 1697 by the Treaty of Ryswick. Renamed Saint Domingue, the new colony rapidly became France's most prosperous colony; it supplied three-fourths of the world's sugar, coffee, and cocoa, and generated more profit than that produced by all the North American colonies together.

In the French half of Hispaniola, the slave trade remained relatively small until 1664, when the French Compagnie des Indes Occidentales began to increase the number of cargo ships transporting Africans to the New World. A study conducted with liberated slave informants revealed that 34 percent were prisoners of war, 30 percent were kidnapped, 7 percent were sold by relatives, 7 percent were sold because of debts, and 11 percent had been condemned to slavery by a judicial process (Reynolds 1985, 33; further data not available). An eleven-year-old boy abducted with his sister by neighbors and sold into slavery reported his horrendous experience of being put in the hold of a slave ship in his memoir written in 1791: "There I received such a salutation in my nostrils as I had never experienced in my life: So that with the loathsomeness of the stench and crying together, I became so sick and low that I was not able to eat" (quoted in Pezzullo 2006, 30).

Women and men between the ages of fourteen and sixty were sent to Saint Domingue ports, separated from their relatives, branded with red-hot irons, and forced to work under grueling conditions in homes or on plantations. Women were particularly vulnerable to rape and sexual abuse by masters and slave drivers. Many were confined in taverns or other settings where prostitution and depravation were rife (Moitt 2001, 99). The significant number of mixed-race children confirms the widespread and systematic sexual assaults of slave girls and women.

By 1700 there were approximately ten thousand slaves in the colony of Saint Domingue, but by the end of the century the estimate had risen to seven hundred thousand. The disparity between the population of slaves and that of whites, who numbered only forty thousand, fostered the threat of revolt and the colonists' increasing intolerance. A planter's daughter wrote: "We are five whites . . . surrounded by over 200 slaves; from morning to night their faces stare at us. . . . Our talk is taken up with the health of slaves, the care they require, their schemes for revolt, and all our lives are bound up with these wretched beings" (quoted in Heinl and Heinl 1978, 33). Colonists' reaction to this state of fear degenerated into abusive practices. The documented excesses of plantation owners included indiscriminate rape and killing and common torture, such as sewing lips together, castration, breast mutilation, and ignition of the anus stuffed with gunpowder. Visitors to the colony also reported that disobedient slaves were crucified, burned alive in large cauldrons, or drowned in weighted sacks in the Saint Domingue bays (Deibert 2006).

Because the colony was embroiled in slavery problems, in 1685 King Louis XIV issued the Proclamation Concerning the Security of the French Islands in America, better known as the Black Code. It provided for due process, limited hours of work, food allotments for slaves, limits on punishment and sexual abuse, and minimal control over the despotic authority of masters. Code protections were largely ignored; the combination of the freedoms granted to slaves and their increasing presence in the country exacerbated the conflicts between races and classes.

Despite domination and abuse, restrictions and curfews, slaves managed to craft their own language—Creole—by combining French, native African dialects, Spanish, and English. They also contrived to maintain their native religious beliefs—known as *vodou*—often practiced secretly underneath the apparent observance of Catholicism imposed by the French. Despite rigid prohibitions, *vodou* was not only a religion but also a vital spiritual force and a source of psychological liberation, which enabled the slaves to survive and afterward empowered them to surmount their oppression.

The volatile mix of social hatred and slaves' resistance was well captured in a 1783 account by a French noble. He portrayed Saint Domingue as a tinderbox ready to erupt: "This colony of slaves is like a city under the imminence of attack; we are treading on loaded barrels of gunpowder" (quoted in Heinl and Heinl 1978, 37). It was the French Revolution that ignited the slaves' anger and nourished their hopes (Dubois 2012, 24). On the night of August 14, 1791, near Cap-Haitien in the north of the country, a *vodou* priest (or *houngan*) named Boukman held a religious ceremony aimed at encouraging slaves to fight for their freedom. One week later, five thousand slaves under the leadership of Boukman began their savage campaign against French domination. Within the first few days, approximately two thousand whites were killed with a barbarism comparable to their treatment of the slaves. Hundreds of plantations were ransacked and destroyed. After a short but bloody suppression of the rebellion by the French, the black army finally prevailed by using the military strategies designed by their new leader, Toussaint L'Ouverture, and in 1793 the surviving white colonists were forced to leave the country.

The liberation from slavery and the independence of the country lasted only until December 1801, when Napoleon deployed twenty-five thousand soldiers in Saint Domingue in efforts to suppress the rebels. However, their resistance and the arms and ammunition provided by President Thomas Jefferson, as well as the scarcity of food, the occurrence of the rainy season in the region, and the resulting proliferation of lethal diseases, including yellow fever, continually decimated the French troops. Despite several attempts by Napoleon to regain the colony and its strategic position in the Caribbean during the following two years, at the end of November 1803, having lost over sixty thousand soldiers, the French finally abandoned Saint Domingue. On January 1, 1804, Toussaint's successor, Jean Jacque Dessalines, proclaimed the island to be an independent republic under the original Arawak name of Haiti. After an estimated loss of 350,000 combatants between 1791 and 1804, Haiti became the first and only republic created by a slave revolt.

The Struggle of Haiti

The bloody war of independence did not lead to the fulfillment of the hopes of the Haitian people. In the years following the recognition of the nation as an independent state, the reins of government passed through the hands of a series of repressive leaders. They established a political culture based on the use of military force, discord within the population, troubled financial planning, and inefficient administration. Contested by different political parties, the nation was split between north and south from 1806 to 1820. An autocratic, but stable and prosperous, northern state contrasted with a more democratic southern system that faced constant financial difficulties (Ballard and Sheehan 1998, 13–16). Reunited in the 1820s, Haiti struggled with the legacy of despotic regimes; internal tensions between north and south, dark and light skin, elites and the poor; and the plague of debt and inefficient administrative control.

Haiti experienced a succession of twenty-one presidents in the seventy years between 1845 and 1915. Characterized by military despotism as well as the capricious attitudes and fiscal irresponsibility of the leaders, these governments continued to aggravate the situation within the country. Economically, Haiti was burdened not only by the internal disparities between north and south, but also by external yokes. France, Great Britain, and the United States shared dominance of Haitian trade by imposing onerous tariffs on goods. In addition, the dependence of the entire economy on the cultivation of coffee, the absence of a marketing policy, the depreciation of the currency, and the reluctance of the elites to invest in the economic development of the country set Haiti on a downward spiral.

Because France had hastily recognized the independence of the colony and had spread the bad reputation of the republic, most European nations considered Haiti to be an "outcast country" and refused to establish diplomatic relations with its representatives. Even the United States and other South American nations did not recognize the Haitian democracy until the middle of the 1860s and refrained from engaging in relations with the successive Haitian governments. However, in 1910, when the nation became insolvent, the United States sought to neutralize European dominance by entering into a common customs receivership of Haitian assets with France and Germany. Given the rising involvement of the United States in the Caribbean region—including the war over Cuba in 1898 and the interest in the Panama Canal in 1903—the United States decided to prevent the country from falling under the control of European powers.

For the same reasons, the Haitian revolt of 1915 against the existing government fostered President Woodrow Wilson's decision to intervene in the island. This first American military incursion into Haitian territory successfully achieved a basis for the security of civilians, established effective communication and cooperation with the Haitian government, developed the infrastructure of the country, and suppressed the revolt without incurring any significant damages. However, such measures failed to encourage long-term investment in economic development, education, or the construction of democratic institutions (Healy 1995, 44). Furthermore, the Americans' racial biases and attempt to outlaw the practice of *vodou* generated profound discontent and disappointment among the population. Criticism and blame replaced the expectations and hopes of the Haitian people.

Intermittent and corrupt regimes followed the departure of the United States from the country in 1934 until François Duvalier, better known as Papa Doc, emerged as the most popular candidate among internal confusion during the national election of 1957. A supporter of the negritude movement and Haitian traditions, including *vodou*, Duvalier established one of the most repressive dictatorships in history. For fourteen years, from 1957 to 1971, Papa Doc dominated the entire country by eliminating potential rivals, prohibiting opposition propaganda and student demonstrations, raping girls and women as a weapon of political intimidation, expelling Catholic priests from the region, and creating his own private security force. The estimated number of Haitians massacred for their opposition or alleged opposition to the regime ranges between thirty thousand and sixty thousand. Meanwhile, thousands of Haitian women, who were fierce resistors as well as victims of the regime, abandoned the country and took refuge in the cities of North America and Europe (Merlet 2002, 160).

Despite the atrocities committed during the Duvalier dictatorship, the United States tolerated it and even sustained the government economically. At that time, global communism was the primary concern in US foreign policy, and Papa Doc's regime, which expressly combated the communist movement, appeared to support US opposition to Fidel Castro in Cuba appropriately. After Duvalier's death in 1971, his son Jean Claude, better known as Baby Doc, inherited power over the country. Convinced that maintaining US support was vital for Haiti and his government, Baby Doc promised the Reagan administration that he would institute economic reforms and improve human rights. However, the internal tensions and the discontent of the population as well as a widespread AIDS epidemic, which affected the entire country and destroyed Haitian tourism, led to the collapse of the Duvalier regime. In 1986 Baby Doc and his family abandoned the country with the support of the United States and were granted asylum by France, and a new military government was established (Ballard and Sheehan 1998, 35–41).

The tremendous problems of Haiti in the late 1980s derived from the unique diplomatic isolation of the country, its poor economic development, the reluctance of rural inhabitants to change, and the absence of an effective system for internal communications. Since the bloody revolution for independence, the United States and France have consistently been the exclusive international players in Haitian affairs, but their participation has often been erratic and invasive and has been aimed primarily at achieving their own interests and gaining their own benefits. Furthermore, the mountainous terrain of the country, the separation between the language of the elites—French—and the language of the poor—Creole—as well as an illiteracy rate of over 70 percent fostered the seclusion of the rural population in hopeless poverty (Rotberg 1988, 93–109).

A multitude of interim governments followed the Duvalier era until the democratic election of the priest Jean-Bertrand Aristide in 1990. As an outspoken critic of the two Duvalier regimes and the subsequent military administrations, Aristide was expelled from the Salesian Order by the Catholic Church in 1988. However, he gained the favor of the Haitian poor—the majority of the country—in sermon after sermon encouraging his parishioners to fight against the privileged classes for a better standard of living. Supported by his Lavalas organization, which means "we will wash away" in Creole, Aristide and his prime minister, René García Préval, established a minimum wage, declared war against corruption and drugs, pursued a literacy campaign, and promoted tourism and investment in the private sector. However, given Artistide's complete lack of political experience, as well as his explicit contempt for the Catholic hierarchy and opposition to the powerful Haitian elites and the military forces, he was rapidly surrounded by many enemies. In 1991, after less than one year in office, Aristide was overthrown in a bloody military coup and forced into exile, first in Venezuela and later in the United States.

The era that followed the subversion of the Aristide's government, from 1991 to 1994, saw a complete breakdown of Haitian civil society and the destruction of any last trace of democracy. Despite the emergence of the new Lavalasian political leader and his innovative regime, the coup demonstrated that the old elites, the Duvalierists, and the armed forces were still extremely influential (Fatton 2002, 77–96). The military junta that supplanted Aristide banned public meetings, violently repressed any sign of political protest, and confiscated the population's assets. Sexual violence against girls and women, particularly gang rape, was among the weapons of political repression employed systematically by the putschists.

The Organization of American States (OAS) and the United Nations officially condemned the military coup and strongly supported Aristide's return to the country. Meanwhile, in order to dislodge the coup leaders, the William Clinton administration imposed a total economic embargo on the island, freezing the Haitian elites' assets held in the United States and shutting down US commercial flights to Haiti. Despite the efforts of the international community, in 1994 it seemed to be clear that diplomatic negotiations, official condemnations, and economic sanctions had failed. For that reason, on July 31, 1994, the United Nations adopted Resolution 940 authorizing a military intervention to remove the coup leaders and to restore Aristide to the presidency.[1] The potential invasion by US troops and diplomatic negotiations by the Clinton administration forced the military junta to resign from power and to consent to the peaceful access of US troops into Haiti and the restoration of Aristide's government.

However, the much-anticipated return of Aristide ended up disappointing the expectations of many supporters of Lavalas. They realized that their leader had become a dangerous demagogue who tolerated no dissent and envisaged creating a new dictatorship based on corruption, political manipulation, and human-rights violations, including widespread and systematic sexual violence against girls and women. At the end of 1995, under international and domestic pressures, Aristide reluctantly declared that he would not run for president again. In 1996, the Lavalas candidate—Préval—Aristide's first prime minister, was inaugurated as the new president of Haiti (Deibert 2006, 48–51).

During Préval's first year in office, twenty-five thousand American soldiers were deployed back into the region to become part of the United

Nations Support Mission in Haiti (UNSMIH), which included approximately thirteen hundred peacekeeping troops and three hundred civilian police whose mandate was to maintain security and political stability in the country. Meanwhile, Aristide announced that he was forming a new political party, Fanmi Lavalas, or the Lavalas Family, which became the machine that would ensure his reelection and ascent to power as well as lead to the downfall of his chosen successor, Préval. Shortly after the formation of the Fanmi Lavalas party, several organizations, called *organizations populaires* (popular organizations) began to spring up as armed political pressure groups in support of the former president of Haiti.

The mutual hostility between Préval and Aristide, the widespread political intimidation, and the increasing street violence that was roiling the country hindered Préval's attempts to effectively govern the state. When the UN mandate for its peacekeeping operation ended in 1997 and the troops left, the UN mission's objectives of peace and stability were far from being achieved. In the following few years, violent confrontations between supporters and opponents of Fanmi Lavalas and brutal assassinations of prominent figures, such as Jean Dominique, the director and owner of the independent Radio Haiti-Inter, continued to paralyze Haiti and thrust the country into anarchy.

In the controversial elections of 2000, in spite of the irregularities and fraudulent manipulations claimed by the international community and the opponents of Fanmi Lavalas, Aristide regained power. Isolated from foreign governments, deprived of international aid, and surrounded by narco-traffickers, criminals, and antidemocratic organizations, Aristide's government transformed Haiti into a pariah nation (Fatton 2002, 141–143). American policymakers began to portray Aristide as a dangerous radical leader and promoted a major denigration campaign against his party. Aristide's opponents, financed by foreign entities, continued to accuse him of corruption, political repression, and gender-based violence. In 2004, the outbreak of violence and the disarray in Haitian communities culminated in the bloody revolt of rebel groups, which erupted in the city of Gonaives, in the north of the country, and rapidly advanced to Port-au-Prince.

Severely condemned by France and the United States, in February 2004, Aristide hastily abandoned Haiti, taking refuge first in the Central African Republic and later in South Africa. Following the ouster of the government, there was a massive breakdown in the poor slum communities that had supported the exiled president's policies. In April 2004, the critical situation of Haiti posed a threat to the peace and security of the entire region. Therefore, the UN Security Council adopted Resolution 1542, establishing MINUSTAH.[2] Despite internal tensions, widespread sexual assaults of girls and women, and violent confrontations among rival armed groups, the interim international peacekeeping government ruled the country until February 2006, when democratic presidential elections declared Préval to be the new president of Haiti.

Further Political Developments

In the following two years, the UN peacekeeping mission focused primarily on providing stabilization and security to the Haitian government as well as supporting the longer process of reforming its key institutions. Indeed, following the successful and peaceful political transition to an elected government, the United Nations continued its strong commitment to the sovereignty, independence, territorial integrity, and unity of Haiti. It envisioned that security, the rule of law and institutional reforms, national reconciliation, and sustainable economic and social development would be fundamental to maintaining the stability of the country.

In particular, the UN mission, in cooperation with the international community, urged the new Haitian government to complete a comprehensive reform of the police, judiciary, and correctional systems. This objective was aimed ultimately at protecting human rights and fundamental freedoms as well as at establishing a fair judicial system and fighting impunity. The United Nations calculated that a firm response to the escalating gang violence, widespread insecurity, and human-rights violations, especially against women and children, was the key to successfully implementing such institutional reforms.[3]

On July 6, 2005, MINUSTAH forces led a full-fledged military attack on Cité Soleil, the slum of Port-au-Prince most affected by armed violence. The target of the military action was the alleged gang leader, Dread Wilme, who was killed during the operation along with an unspecified number of his associates. In response to the high-pitched criticism expressed by international NGOs operating in the country, MINUSTAH acknowledged that the military action had carried with it the collateral risk of civilian casualties and unintended targets. Indeed, UN representatives had warned the Haitian government, the international community, as well as civil society organizations of collateral damage because of the flimsy construction of houses in Cité Soleil and the nature of such missions conducted in densely populated urban areas. The death toll was estimated at close to thirty people. Further, MSF, operating at a nearby hospital, reported treating twenty-six gunshot victims, twenty of whom were women and at least one of whom was a child.

In line with this military operation, on December 22, 2006, MINUSTAH launched another large-scale attack on the residents of Cité Soleil. Again, there were hundreds of peacekeepers present, with aerial support, to confront the relentless armed groups that controlled the area. Once more, the goal of the attack was to apprehend gang members. The ICRC coordinator caustically reported that the UN soldiers prevented Red Cross vehicles from entering the zone to assist wounded women and children. According to MINUSTAH representatives at least nine civilians were killed. However, independent sources estimated that over twenty people were killed and more than forty individuals were reported injured. Other estimates counted up to seventy victims.

A report of the Security Council mission to Haiti (United Nations Security Council 2009, 2) stated that, in the previous few years, positive progress had been made in the overall security situation because of strategic military actions conducted by MINUSTAH with the cooperation of the Haitian National Police. In spite of such interventions, which were aimed at dismantling some of the armed gangs responsible for much of the violence in the capital, criminal activities, insecurity, and gender-based violence remained generally rampant. Instances of civil unrest involving violence usually affected the entire country, undermining public confidence.

The establishment of Préval's elected government in 2006 was a democratic development unprecedented in the political history of Haiti. For the first time, opposing factions and a critical press had the freedom to express their positions and opinions without fear of retaliation and prosecution. Nevertheless, profound divisions within Haitian society and latent political tensions among diverse contending groups undermined the stability of Haiti's democratic institutions. Indeed, relations between the Parliament and the executive branch remained fractured, and their intention to cooperate and reach agreement on several joint legislative and reform agendas was not carried out.

During 2008, further political uncertainty arose from the presidential announcement that eight elections would take place over the subsequent thirty-six months. In the first round of elections, for the renewal of one-third of the Senate, the Provisional Electoral Council rejected the Fanmi Lavalas candidates, who supported the previous president, Aristide. Representatives of political and civil society organizations emphasized the potential for renewed social unrest and confrontations. In response, the Provisional Electoral Council and the United Nations promised free, fair, and inclusive elections. However, several political parties decided to withdraw their participation due, at least in part, to financial constraints.

On a positive note, during Préval's presidency, commissions on education, competitiveness, information technology, security forces, and constitutional reform were established. Political parties, the private sector, and civil society were invited to engage in a constructive dialogue on these fundamental issues in order to restore public confidence in the political process and to ensure the future of the country. In particular, Haitian political leaders and representatives of MINUSTAH indicated that reforming the Constitution was essential for improving the functioning of Haiti's democratic institutions, and, thus, for effecting better governance in the country. Despite such intentions, internal divisions, the onerous administrative structure, and the lack of coordination and imbalance of power between the executive and legislative branches of the government hampered the commissions' ability to deliver concrete results and implement the reform process in the country. *After research ended*

New presidential and legislative elections were originally scheduled for the end of February 2010. However, because of the earthquake that struck Haiti in January 2010, they were repeatedly postponed. Meanwhile, both Baby Doc Duvalier and Aristide returned to the country, a devastating cholera outbreak followed the natural disaster, and acts of violence and voter-fraud allegations marred the electoral process. Finally, at the end of March 2011, the presidential runoff between the popular singer Michel Martelly and the former first lady of Haiti Mirlande Manigat took place. In the end, Martelly won the election for his party, Repons Peyizan

(Farmers' Response Party), and he assumed the position of president on May 14, 2011.

Social Context

Haiti's history of political instability and violence, its poor governance, and the recurrent deterioration of security severely hamper the country's economic growth and development. The detrimental impact of political conflicts, the intermittent cycles of foreign assistance followed by the withdrawal of international aid, and the high degree of inequitable and inadequate access to productive assets and public services make the country the poorest in the Latin American and Caribbean region and the most disadvantaged in the Western Hemisphere (World Bank 2006b). About 54 percent of the entire Haitian population of nearly eight million lives below the US$1-a-day poverty line and 78 percent below US$2-a-day (World Bank 2006a). Large pockets of urban indigence in the slum areas of Port-au-Prince, including Martissant, Gran Ravine, Carrefour, Cité Soleil, and Bel Air, register even higher poverty rates.

Every day, in the smothering tropical heat and dampness, thousands of girls and women endure the long and exhausting journey from their shantytowns to the markets or rich areas of the city. A market seller's daily wage amounts to barely US$1, and the average monthly salary of a household servant is about US$20 (Maternowska 2006, 1). Girls as young as twelve to fifteen years old work as prostitutes along the main roads of Port-au-Prince and earn around US$0.68 in a normal workday. The level of poverty in the country can also be measured by the illiteracy rate: 90 percent of the Haitian population speaks only Creole, and less than 39.5 percent can read; only 55 percent of children between the ages of six and twelve are enrolled in school, with a larger proportion being males (World Bank 2006b).

Particularly during 2008, the food crisis, the global financial and economic collapse, and the devastating impact of the hurricane season had adverse effects on the socioeconomic situation in Haiti. According to a postdisaster needs assessment conducted with the assistance of the World Bank, the European Union, and the United Nations, the 2008 storms and hurricanes resulted in some US$900 million worth of damage, the equivalent of 14.6 percent of Haiti's gross domestic product (United Nations Security Council 2009, 10).

Degradation and lack of infrastructure, including basic services such as potable water, electricity, and sanitation, characterize the wretched living conditions of the slums' inhabitants and exacerbate their anger and discontent. Persistent poverty and youth unemployment in urban communities engender an environment that is susceptible to civil unrest and gang activity. Indeed, controlled by rival armed groups splintered from the Lavalasian organizations and their opponents, the poor communities become the setting for rapes and slaughters. While terror erupts, girls and women scream, and people starve, "hungry pigs . . . [discover] bodies stashed behind buildings or buried shallowly in the open trash pits, . . . evidence of the crimes committed" (Maternowska 2006, 8).

Poverty, violence, and insecurity also foster the conditions that allow children to become homeless orphans; they are forcibly recruited by the armed groups to carry heavy loads of looted goods and to fight as soldiers on the front line. For girls, armed groups represent the inescapable threat of rape, sexual slavery, and forced prostitution. Danise, a twenty-two-year-old former resident of Cité Soleil, confirmed that "young girls are often raped by the members of the rival gang as a way of reprisal" (quoted in United Nations International Children's Emergency Fund 2006). A study conducted by the MINUSTAH Gender Unit and the United Nations Development Programme (UNDP) in Haiti revealed that the armed groups, which sweep the slum neighborhoods and exert control over the population, comprise mostly children, adolescents, and young adults between the ages of ten and twenty-five (United Nations Stabilization Mission in Haiti and United Nations Development Programme in Haiti 2006). Women and girls are also involved in the armed factions, as combatants or partners of members, prostitutes, or sex slaves.

Most of the participants in armed violence are sociopolitically motivated either to fight for social change or to take part in organized crime. Among the active armed groups, the distinction between political motivation and organized crime is often blurred. Indeed, political objectives are normally not clear because of the numerous clandestine criminal and violent activities that are perpetrated by these groups while they are allegedly advancing a political platform or socially legitimate interest. For instance, drug trafficking is one of the principal profitable illegal activities conducted by Haitian gangs. The UN mission has described its corruptive influence in Haiti as one of the most serious factors destabilizing the country and undermining the sustainability of its security (United Nations Stabilization Mission in Haiti and United Nations Development Programme in Haiti 2006).

Despite their different risk factors, structures, and dynamics, the armed groups in Haiti can be broadly placed into the following categories (United Nations General Assembly/Security Council 2006). The Milices Populaires (popular organizations) comprise primarily young men and some former members of security forces. These groups control the territory of deprived communities in Port-au-Prince, including Martissant, Cité Soleil, and Bel Air. Supporters of the Lavalas party, the Popular Organizations were established in the late 1980s as sociopolitical associations to organize resistance in the final years of the Duvalier dictatorship. Later, during Aristide's regime, these organizations were converted into associations that distributed resources from the state to the communities. These armed groups are responsible for the recruitment of women as well as for the perpetration of rape and sexual violence against them as a weapon of war and as retaliation against rival factions.

The *organisations politiques* (political organizations) are armed groups that are politically motivated. Their political positions depend on the role of their respective leaders. Nevertheless, tension exists within those political organizations that also operate as popular organizations as they oscillate between these two different groups. Which of these activities they carry out depends on the advantages that each activity can bring. Members of the political organizations use large-caliber weapons. Women and girls are not targeted and are not recruited as members of the groups.

The armed groups called paramilitaries (Front de Résistance) include, instead, former members of the military, excommunicated members of the Haitian police, and civilians who overthrew Aristide's government in 2004 and contested the elections of February 2006 as a national political front (Front de Reconstruction Nationale). Located primarily in Gonaives, the paramilitaries are a political opposition group involved in illicit activities, such as extortion and banditry, and they are also responsible for rape and sexual violence against girls and women.

The Baz Arm are gangs that consist mostly of adolescents involved in organized crime. Based on the personal interests of their members, such as sports, cultural activities, and political reunions, these associations end up being exploited by the popular organizations to perform criminal tasks, including trafficking weapons and drugs. Similarly, the armed criminal gangs are involved in organized crime. The establishment of these gangs is a direct consequence of the deterioration in the standard of living, high unemployment rates, poor governance, and proliferating armed confrontations in the city. Rape and sexual assaults against girls and women serve as rewards for their illegal operations.

The vagabond gangs generally comprise children and adolescents who perpetrate widespread and systematic gang rapes against girls in order to control their conduct and impose macho values within their communities. Vagabond gangs use light weapons to carry out punitive gang rapes and to terrorize their victims. Finally, the Brigades de Vigilance (vigilante groups) are aggressive self-defense associations; teenagers and adults join these groups in response to escalating violence and criminality in slum communities. Group members aim to defend their immediate environment against other bandits, gangsters, robbers, and rapists. Women serve as active members of these groups to defend specific areas.

References to these different armed groups and their acts of gender-based violence as well as their recruitment of Haitian women and girls will be made throughout this book. Following the above discussion of the historical roots for sexual violence and female retaliation in Haiti, the next chapter addresses the prevalence of gender-based violence worldwide and particularly in Haiti. It describes specific practices of discrimination and sexual violence affecting girls and women both in the private realm and in the public sphere. Poignant testimonies of victims as well as of institutional representatives of international, national, and civil society organizations accompany and facilitate the relevant analysis.

2

Gender-Based Violence in Haiti

Statistics here useful for media
Portfolio

Many studies have thoroughly documented the prevalence of violence against women in both industrialized and less-developed societies. A population-based survey conducted in ten countries, including data from over twenty-four thousand informants around the world, revealed that the lifetime chance of physical violence affecting a woman over the age of fifteen ranged from less than 10 percent in Ethiopia, Japan, Serbia, and Montenegro to 62 percent in Samoa (World Health Organization 2005, 43). The chance of sexual violence being perpetrated against a woman over fifteen years of age varied from less than 1 percent in Ethiopia and Bangladesh to between 10 percent and 12 percent in Peru, Samoa, and the United Republic of Tanzania (World Health Organization 2005, 45). Overall, the data revealed that between 19 percent and 76 percent of women around the world had suffered from physical and sexual violence by an intimate partner or a nonpartner since the age of fifteen.

Proportional data estimated that, among women who had been physically or sexually assaulted since the age of fifteen, from 60 percent to 80 percent, meaning over two-thirds of them, had been abused by an intimate partner (World Health Organization 2005, 46). Specific data showed that the lifetime chance of physical violence being inflicted by a partner varied between 13 percent and 61 percent from country to country, with the average falling between 23 percent and 49 percent (United Nations 2006, 43). The lifetime chance of sexual violence being perpetrated by an intimate partner ranged from 6 percent to 59 percent, with the rate in most countries falling between 10 percent and 50 percent. Physical and sexual assaults often overlapped with emotionally abusive behavior, which affected between 10 percent and 75 percent of women. Even in industrialized countries such as France and Germany, national studies revealed that 35 percent and 49 percent of women, respectively, had experienced intimidating and emotional aggression by intimate partners (United Nations 2006, 44–45).

The chance of sexual abuse being perpetrated against girls younger than fifteen years of age ranged from 1 percent in Bangladesh to 21 percent in Namibia (World Health Organization 2005, 49). Forced sexual initiation affected between 9 percent of girls (in the United States) and 40 percent (in Peru) (United Nations 2006, 49). A Canadian study among teenagers between the ages of fifteen and nineteen revealed that 54 percent of the girls had been sexually coerced in a dating relationship. Findings from the United States in 2000 showed that 22 percent of girls in high school and 32 percent in college had experienced dating violence. Furthermore, about 8.3 percent of women in the United States had been physically or sexually assaulted by a dating partner, and 20.6 percent experienced more than one type of dating violence (World Health Organization 2005, 49). Especially in less developed countries with high rates of HIV/AIDS and other sexually transmitted diseases, young girls may face sexual coercion in exchange for food, money, school fees, or little gifts.

The rest of this chapter presents findings and testimonies related to specific practices of gender-based violence in the Haitian context, including domestic violence and child slavery as well as political and gang rape. The empirical analysis is supported by a theoretical examination of common patterns of gender imbalance and violence against women and girls. The chapter also explores the connection between female subjugation and abuse in both the private and the public spheres.

The Normalization of Gender-Based Violence in Haiti

This research study was conducted in the urban slums of Haiti, where available data suggested a high prevalence of sexual violence against girls and women. In the shantytowns of Port-au-Prince, which are characterized by armed violence among rival gangs, an estimated 50 percent

50% — half

of girls have been victims of rape, often by more than one perpetrator (United Nations General Assembly/Security Council 2006). A study of the factors affecting youth development in Haiti revealed that violence is part of everyday life and that sexual violence is rampant: 46 percent of Haitian girls have been sexually abused, among whom 33 percent are between five and nine years of age and 43 percent between ten and fourteen (Justesen and Verner 2007, 4). Findings from a random survey of households in Port-au-Prince suggested that, between 2004 and 2006, thirty-five thousand women were sexually assaulted, half of whom were under the age of eighteen (Kolbe and Hutson 2006). Aggregated figures show that sexual violence against women is the most prevalent form of violence in Haiti, affecting 35 percent of women over fifteen years of age with a higher incidence in provincial areas (41 percent) than in urban settings (34 percent) (World Bank 2006b, 33).

Disaggregated data collected for the purpose of this study from civil society organizations that provide medical and psychological assistance to victims of sexual violence in Haiti show that the number of rape cases per annum increased between threefold and twelvefold from 2002 to 2005. Among the victims, 96.1 percent were single women, and between 34 percent and 76.1 percent were girls under eighteen years of age (Table de Concertation Nationale sur les Violences Faites aux Femmes 2005b). One organization operating in Port-au-Prince described the prevalence of sexual violence in the conflict areas of the capital: 63 percent of rape cases occurred after intimidation with a firearm, 71 percent were committed by strangers, and between 41 percent and 62 percent were committed by more than one perpetrator (Table de Concertation Nationale sur les Violences Faites aux Femmes 2005b). Estimates of the prevalence of sexual violence in 2006 ranged from 64 percent in Port-au-Prince to 69 percent throughout the entire country. Among the victims, 65 percent were girls between the ages of three and eighteen, 17 percent were between nineteen and twenty-five years of age, and 16 percent were over twenty-six. Among the rape cases documented, 53 percent were committed by armed groups and 29 percent by more than one of their members (Kay Fanm 2007; SOFA, 2007).

Several authors have examined patterns of risk factors for sexual violence in Haiti. A number of studies have discussed the interplay between political violence and forced sex since the Haitian military coup in 1991–1994 (Magloire 2004; Merlet 2002, 160). Widely employed as a weapon of political oppression, rape against women has remained since then deeply embedded in Haitian society, shaping gender relationships in both private and public spheres. Correlations between practices of gender discrimination and sexual abuse in the private realm and gender-based violence in the public domain have also been suggested (Faedi 2008). Other studies acknowledge the challenges of Haitian women in both rural and impoverished urban settings; they are often forced by extreme poverty and gender inequality to become entangled in survival strategies, including abusive relationships or trading sex for food, money, and protection (Maternowska 2006; Smith Fawzi et al. 2005).

The disturbing figures on sexual violence against women reported in the international organizations' policy papers and institutional documents mirror the data provided by civil society organizations. Even so, the incidence of violence affecting women is probably higher than has been documented. Indeed, the UN Special Rapporteur on violence against women, on a mission to Haiti in 2000, estimated that over 66 percent of rape victims never report the aggression for fear of reprisal and social stigmatization (United Nations Economic and Social Council 2000). The interviews conducted for the purpose of this research revealed conflicting data. Representatives of international organizations operating in the country reported a significant enhancement of security, suggesting an improvement in women's safety as well, after the UN military interventions of December 2006 in the conflict areas of Port-au-Prince. However, interviews with victims revealed that rape and sexual violence are still widespread and systematically perpetrated, although in a more secretive way.

When asked whether the UN military operations aimed at disbanding the armed groups in some shantytowns of the capital had made any difference, a young woman from one of the neighborhoods responded sadly: "Yes, the only difference is that now the gangs don't fight against each other during the day. But at night they keep doing whatever they want. . . . They rape women and girls, sometime even babies. . . . This is the only difference. You can say that there is no war in the streets right now, but still they bring the war to the houses. Nothing changes in these places, you know. . . . Bandits keep raping as it was before." Such data inconsistency may occur both because rape victims do not report the aggression to competent authorities and because violence against women has become normalized. A representative of IBERS in Cap-Haitien crystallized this depraved custom in this way: "*le viol est comme le bonjour,*" meaning that rape is so widely and habitually committed that is like saying "good morning" every day.

Studies have acknowledged the normalization of violence in Haitian society, reporting that over 58 percent of residents in the metropolitan areas feel unsafe in their own homes and that women, in particular, are the primary target of the assaults (World Bank 2006b, 12). A young woman recounted her experience with violence during an interview.

INTERVIEWEE: I was home with my little brothers and sisters and my mom was at work at that time of the afternoon. An armed man forced the door and invaded the house. He was looking for money, but I did not have any and he got really upset.

INTERVIEWER: Did you know this man?

INTERVIEWEE: Yes, he is one of the leaders of a gang. I knew that the money was just an excuse. He wanted more. . . . In fact, he started threatening to rape my two-year-old little sister. I was out of my mind and I started begging him to save my sisters and brothers and to take me instead. I didn't know what else to do. . . . I didn't want to go through the same pain and nightmare, but I couldn't do anything else. I had to save the children.

INTERVIEWER: What happened then?

INTERVIEWEE: He accepted my offer to rape me instead of my little sister. I begged him to do it in another room because I didn't want the children to see me. He consented. I took him in the other room and I closed my eyes while he was over me. I couldn't even cry because I did not want to scare the kids.

The majority of women interviewed confirmed their powerlessness when facing armed men as well as their steadfast belief that any response to violence would be useless. "When armed men want you, there is nothing you can do but cover your eyes and wait [until] the moment passes by," a fifty-three-year-old victim stated loudly in one of the focus-group encounters. Another declared: "Armed men just want to take advantage of beautiful girls . . . but they also rape old women just for fun and disrespect. You know, they can do whatever they want and have whomever they want, even very young girls or babies, because they have guns. Guns mean power, and, above all, being a man means having power over women."

Gender disparities clearly emerged from women's accounts. Most of them seemed to passively accept their condition, confiding hopelessly that "women can only be victims, victims of everything." Others became very quiet when the focus-group discussions moved from violence committed by armed gangs to the general understanding of women's role in society and, particularly, in the household. However, the most loquacious women frankly claimed that their status as victims had very little to do with being raped by gangs, but rather it commenced in their childhood when inequality and sexual abuse became their very first memories. One reflected: "I was first raped when I was so small that I could not even count my age. That's my first memory. When I was raped many years later by three armed men one after the other, it did not even hurt anymore. It was just the same memory all over again."

Representatives of civil society organizations interviewed for the purpose of this study confirmed that girls experience sexual initiation at the age of five or six, primarily with relatives or neighbors. In particular, one psychologist working for rape victims' rehabilitation programs revealed the lack of boundaries among family members and the discrimination, neglect, and concealed incest that affect girls behind closed doors. Another interviewee, who was providing psychological support to rape victims, explained that women are so accustomed to sexual abuse that by now they have accepted violence as part of their daily lives, simply resigning themselves to their unfortunate condition.

Gender Inequality and Domestic Violence in Haiti

In Haiti, the household is the first domain in which power, authority, and conflict define the contours of gender relations (Maternowska 2006, 44). It is behind the family door that cultural beliefs and rules, misery and violence, loss and love generate power-imbalance relationships between men and women. Strategies for survival shape the gender disparity of responsibilities, resources, and possibilities that embed themselves in the practices of discrimination and often degenerate into the sexual abuse and slavery of girls and women. Inequality and violence perpetrated inside the household ultimately impair girls' and women's status within the Haitian social hierarchies and generate patterns of gender-based violence in the public sphere.

Haitian shanties are constructed using rudimentary materials, including cement blocks and wooden planks, and are topped with tin plates that trap the burning rays of the sun. They usually have one or two rooms where as many as twelve people live, adults and children together. Very poorly furnished and humid inside, they are often only partially locked and are dark for lack of electricity. Given the cramped living spaces, easily accessible to neighbors and strangers, "sleeping in Haiti is dangerous" (Maternowska 2006, 46). Informants unanimously revealed that girls' first sexual contacts begin at the age of five or six and are experienced primarily with relatives or neighbors.

They also confirmed that Haitian society is imbued with a culture of violence. As a result, the sexual assault of girls and women inside the household is the product of customary norms of repression against the vulnerable and the inferior. As in many other patriarchal societies, Haitian marital unions are informed by the model of a male breadwinner and a female caregiver (Freedman 2002, 124). Primarily responsible for domestic duties, including washing, preparing food, and caring for children, women look to men, almost exclusively, for economic support. The daily struggle for survival forces women to choose their partners for their most basic assets—good health and the ability to work—which will eventually provide security and income for the household.

Given these societal standards and the constrained means for living, sexual relationships are structured primarily on gender-based contracts and expectations. In the realm of sexuality, women's concern for financial gain becomes men's power and gives them legitimacy to dictate conjugal rules, mistreat their partners, and engage in polygamy. Informants revealed that women's economic dependence is the primary cause of their subordination and submission within the family or relationships. It is commonly and customarily accepted that men will make decisions in the household, sexually abuse their partners, and maintain several unions with different women concurrently. In contrast, women and girls are expected to be tamed by men for their own good "either by word or blow" in the event that they interrupt the domestic peace by disobedience (Freedman 2002, 293).

A sociology professor at the University of Port-au-Prince who was interviewed for this study found that Haitian women often suffer from two types of violence within the household: structural violence, which is the violence perpetrated through psychological, physical, or emotional acts of aggression; and symbolic violence, which occurs when their husbands abandon them either to join the gangs or, more frequently, to engage in multiple extramarital relationships. In the city, men who are unemployed usually leave their partners to avoid their financial and parental responsibilities. In the countryside, men often have several families concurrently: one in each place where they own a strip of land.

Childbearing and motherhood are women's major sources of bargaining power in relationships, even though they generally become their own load and plight. Participants recalled the popular Haitian proverb "*ti moun se riches pòv malèrè*"—children are the wealth of the poor—but a Cité Soleil resident also declared: "When a man gives you a child now, he leaves, without even looking back. It's a huge injustice. You wish that he had killed you instead. And when you're pregnant, I don't need to tell you about the hunger, bare feet on the ground, everything in your body cries out" (Maternowska 2006, 44).

Cultural beliefs and patriarchal values as well as a hand-to-mouth existence reinforce the idea that the purpose of having children is to promote the economy of the household. Girls as young as five years of age are expected to carry water, prepare food, wash dishes and clothes, help sell in the markets, and go on errands for their relatives. Representatives of the Ministry for the Status of Women interviewed for the purpose of this study declared that even poverty in Haiti is gendered. Females are fed less than their male counterparts, are forced to work harder, are given less schooling, and are denied equal access to medical care.

While parents toil outside the house and brothers are often given preferential opportunities to attend school or to take apprenticeships, girls as young as seven or eight years old are charged with watching younger siblings and working inside the home. Behind closed doors, because of the obliviousness of the parents and the complacency of spectators and other responsible adults, sexual abuse and violence against girls take place undisturbed. Because chastity and a virtuous reputation are prerequisites for marriage, which is females' principal goal and their only means of subsistence, sexual violations against them, especially if committed by relatives, intimates, or neighbors, often remain a secret matter within the family involved. Representatives of UNICEF Haiti, as participants in this study, recalled the case of a minor who, after being raped by her stepfather, was abandoned by her own mother and eventually blamed by the entire community for divulging the aggression.

Another horrifying story was reported by a nun who is the head of a Cité Soleil religious institution that provides shelter, food, schooling, and vocational training to girls living in the area, most of whom have been sexually abused:

> Malya is fifteen years old and is one of our best students. She has been attending our school for several years. Her mother had a small business here in Cité Soleil, but she got a lot of debts and did not know how to pay them back. Over a year ago, she ran off and left Malya with her godmother and her husband. The girl has been living with them since then. About a week ago, during a class, Malya lamented to one of our Sisters that she was not feeling well. She had pain in her abdomen and she was hardly able to walk. The Sister took the girl to our infirmary. After a medical exam, they called me urgently. Malya had been brutally raped by the husband of her godmother for about a year. Her vagina was completely lacerated, disfigured by a fungal infection, and covered with excrescences all around it. I was horrified and I could not help closing my eyes at such a terrible sight. Afterward, I took Malya's face in my hands and asked her: "How can a man keep raping you in such a state? How is it possible?" The girl then told me that the man used to cover her mouth with a bandage to keep the neighbors from hearing her screams while he was sexually abusing her.

After this episode, the nun decided to call Malya's mother and inform her of the repetitive acts of violence committed against her daughter. The woman replied that the fact that the man was sexually enjoying Malya's favors was a good way to repay him and his wife for looking after the girl. She also declared that it was none of the nun's business to interfere in another family's private matters. The nun was horrified and decided to take Malya away from her godmother's house and host her in the organization's shelter.

In Haiti, as in other patriarchal societies, a girl's body is one of the very few possessions that even poor parents can claim as their own and defend as private property. Because women's offspring are a commodity to be transferred from fathers to their daughters' husbands and the paternity of the children needs to be ensured, girls have to be chaste before marriage and have to remain faithful after it (Lerner 1986). Almost never reported because of social expectations and the fear of stigmatization, domestic sexual abuse and violence against girls are generally perceived as unfortunate events of life rather than as crimes against the integrity of the victims' bodies.

Social pressure and economic needs also foster the conditions that encourage girls to mate after puberty: by the age of seventeen, 19 percent of all Haitian girls have already had their first baby or are pregnant, and the rate increases to 31 percent by the time they are nineteen years old (Maternowska 2006, 46). Teenage mothers account for 8 percent of all births in the country and contribute to Haiti's high fertility rate of approximately 4.2 children per woman. Because of the lack of heath care, information, and family counseling, contraceptive usage is among the lowest in the Western Hemisphere and HIV/AIDS has reached epidemic levels—the highest prevalence in Latin America and the Caribbean region and, indeed, the highest incidence outside Africa. Among fifteen-to-nineteen-year olds, 5.2 percent of the population is afflicted with HIV/AIDS. Teenage pregnancies and HIV/AIDS are seen primarily in girls from low-income households and deprived communities (Justesen and Verner 2007, 4). Sexual survival strategies and low use of condoms as well as patterns of sexual abuse and gender inequality significantly affect women's possibility to negotiate with their partners and effectively protect themselves.

The Practice of Restavèk

In Haiti the patriarchal misconception of the female body as property generates a specific kind of exploitation against children—*restavèk*, meaning "to stay with" in Creole. Around one out of ten children from ten to seventeen years old is engaged in domestic work away from their families. Girls account for 75 percent of the 300,000 Haitian child workers sent, out of desperation by indigent parents, to work as domestic help in richer households (United Nations International Children's Emergency Fund 2006). Families, especially in rural areas, who barely eke out a subsistence living on the economic margins and are unable to feed or educate their numerous offspring sell children for a few *gourdes* to wealthier families living in urban communities.[1]

Prospective employers typically visit the birth parents and promise to feed, educate, and care for their restavèks in exchange for domestic help. However, transferred as a commodity from one family to another, girls, in most cases, end up being sexually abused and exploited, coerced into slavery and overwork, and given meager food rations and limited possibilities for receiving an education. As an example of this practice, a report from the United Nations International Children's Emergency Fund (2006) tells the story of Celine, a thirteen-year-old girl who was sexually abused and severely burned by the men who owned her.

The parish priest of a Catholic church in a slum of Port-au-Prince, Martissant, who is the director of a program for child restavèks, reported the following case:

> Carline is only five years old but she already knows how difficult life is. Every morning, she climbs a hill in Petionville [a district of Port-au-Prince], carrying a huge drum full of water on her head. She walks almost three miles every day to get water from the public fountain. Carline was born in the countryside outside the small town of Hinche in the north of the country. Her parents were extremely poor and decided to send her away to work as a domestic servant for some distant relatives in the Haitian capital. Ever since, Carline has been responsible for securing water for the family, looking after the children, cleaning the house, doing the laundry, and preparing meals. She does not have any time left to go to school or to play with other children. At night, she sleeps on the floor in the kitchen; and if she has done something wrong, she is then forced to sleep standing up as punishment.

"The child restavèk are treated like dogs, sometimes even worse than dogs in Haiti," the parish priest declared during the interview. Still, he acknowledged that a further challenge is the fact that most of these children come from such poor communities that they do not even have birth certificates. The lack of identification documents inevitably facilitates their exploitation and, sometimes, disappearance. The situation often degenerates when restavèks reach the age of fifteen. Indeed, although, according to the current law, they should then be employed and paid for their services, the hosting families usually either abandon them on the street or keep them working for free (Sommerfelt 2002).

The Special Rapporteur on violence against women, reporting on the mission to Haiti in 2000, stated that young girls working as restavèks are often at the mercy of their employers and that the high incidence of sexual violence resulting in pregnancy is of serious concern (United Nations Economic and Social Council, 2000). More recently, a random survey of 1,260 households (5,720 individuals) in Port-au-Prince revealed that, during the twenty-two-month period following the departure of Aristide in 2004, thirty-five thousand women were sexually assaulted, half of whom were under the age of eighteen (Kolbe and Hutson 2006). In particular, the study reported that female restavèks accounted for a substantial portion (36.2 percent) of all sexual violence victims; 9.6 percent of all girl restavèks had been sexually abused; and the rate of sexual assault for female restavèks was 4.5 greater than that for girls who were not restavèks.

Advocates in the program mentioned above for restavèks at the Catholic church in Martissant who were interviewed for the purpose of this research declared that because female restavèks are perceived as being the property of the household, they are often raped and sexually abused by their employers in a context of full impunity. Fear of reprisal and social stigmatization as well as the ineffectiveness of the criminal legal system prevent victims from reporting the aggression. A culture of neglect and abuse toward children, particularly girls, informs Haitian society, and violence is widely employed as a method of imparting education and discipline. Poverty and the lack of solidarity among indigent families as well as the widespread culture of exploitation and enslavement of girls are the primary root causes of the practice of restavèk.

For instance, Marje, a twelve-year-old girl from a rural area, reported her experience of restavèk working for two different families in Port-au-Prince:

> I have worked for two households. At the beginning I was a restavèk
> for a family in Delmas where they maltreated me, injured me, and
> battered me as if I was a dog. When my master was angry he forced
> me to raise my arms against the wall and maimed me so hard that I
> almost fainted. He left me without food until the next day, . . . and he
> let me sleep standing on my feet. I ran away and became a restavèk
> for another family where I suffered again much pain. . . . I would love
> to go back to my parents or at least to see them once and then come
> back to Port-au-Prince and find another family where I can carry out
> domestic work proportional to my strength, such as preparing food
> or cleaning the home. . . . But more than anything I want go to school.

After being repeatedly raped by her master, Marje eventually got pregnant
and was abandoned on a street. Participants in this research from UNICEF
Haiti highlighted the fact that female restavèks are relegated to secondary citizenship status, which makes them vulnerable to sexual exploitation
and abuse, as well as depriving them of basic human rights.

Generally considered to be a modern-day form of child slavery, the
practice of restavèk recalls the harshness toward and atrocities committed
against girl slaves at the time of French colonialism, as described in Chapter I. The colonialists left, but the psychological implications connected
to their domination have been deeply absorbed in Haitian culture. Rich
men have power and money to enslave the poor and women. Some writers
have indeed connected child domestic labor in Haiti to the historic legacy
of slavery (Cadet 1998). Implicit in this argument is the fact that slavery
and, thus, violence and abuse form part of Haiti's cultural heritage and,
therefore, are highly tolerated.

Since independence, the practice of restavèk has been continually
employed and has contributed significantly to the massive migration
from the rural provinces to Port-au-Prince (see generally Haitian Ministry of Social Affaires 2002). Whereas, initially, the hosting families were
relatively wealthy and educated, nowadays only modest and disadvantaged
households rely on the domestic help of restavèks. Starvation, the demo-
graphic expansion, and the migratory movements toward urban communities entrap birth families and girls into a downward spiral of slavery,
abuse, and sexual violence.

A representative of the IOM in Port-au-Prince who participated in this study claimed that until recently the Haitian government did not even acknowledge the extent of the restavèk problem. Some officials still argue that this is a traditional practice used by poor families to give their children a better chance in life. But the international community has refused to accept such an interpretation by declaring that the practice of restavèk is a real form of child slavery.

According to representatives of UNICEF interviewed for this study, the number of restavèks has doubled in recent years, as poverty, distress, and poor governance continue to oppress the Haitian countryside. Moreover, during the interview conducted for the purpose of this study, a representative of IOM emphasized that in 2008 the IOM registered increasing trafficking of restavèks across the border between Haiti and the Dominican Republic, on the eastern side of the island. Indeed, because economic conditions are much better there, many poor Haitian families hope to help their children by handing them over to agents who ferry them across the border. However, once on the other side, without documents and legal rights, these children often end up being exploited and abused by hosting families. In addition, girls frequently become victims of sex trafficking and prostitution.

Political Rape

The inequality and sexual violence perpetrated against girls and women inside the household and within their intimate relationships gravitate into the public sphere, where they trace patterns of gender-based violence and leave Haitian society in misery and distress. Whether expressed through patriarchy, sexual stereotypes, male dominance, or female subordination, power lies at the very core of gender disparities and strains (Hirschon 1984, 1). In Haiti, where poverty, instability, and violence contaminate the history and impede the development of the country, and where politics and power viciously intertwine, practices of gender-based violence become tools for political confrontations and repression as well.

No proper understanding and analysis of the systematic rape of girls as a political weapon can be made without examining closely the period of the military regime from 1991 to 1994, when acts of sexual violence against

girls and women informed the regular political strategy aimed at controlling and terrorizing the entire population (Merlet 2002, 160). Already
employed during the two Duvalier dictatorships, widespread and systematic rape for political purposes culminated in 1991, when the leaders of the
Haitian army overthrew the regime of Aristide, leading the country toward
war and public disorder.

In particular, following the military coup, *zenglendos*, or thugs, burst
into houses at any time, raping and beating girls and women. This became
a common method of putting political pressure on and perpetrating violence against the opponents of the regime. Approximately 1,680 girls and
women who were either themselves prodemocracy supporters or relatives
of supporters were brutalized and victims of political rape (United Nations
Social and Economic Council 2000). The report of the Special Rapporteur
on violence against women on the mission to Haiti in 2000 collected some
of their stories. The following one is typical (United Nations Social and
Economic Council 2000, 16):

> On 13 February 1993, a group of armed men came into the house
> where Esperance was living with her parents, who were political
> activists. They created disorder in the house, raped her nineteen-
> year-old sister in front of her, beat her and her brothers, beat her
> mother, beat her father and took him away. Esperance has not seen
> her father again. Esperance fled to a southern province. When her
> mother died in 1995, traumatized by the loss of her husband, Esper-
> ance had to leave school to take care of her younger siblings. Since
> they had no permanent place to live, her family is now dispersed,
> the siblings living temporarily wherever they find a place. . . . Her
> sister still suffers from serious medical conditions as a consequence
> of the rape ("le corps se souvient"—the body remembers).

During the Haitian coup of 1991–1994, when widespread repression
and violence created circumstances akin to war, the perpetration of rape
as a punitive and intimidating weapon against the opposing political
factions resembled the brutalization committed in wartime (Magloire
2004). Participants in this study contended that the outbreak of violence that engulfed communities and generated gender-based assaults,

including gang rape and battery, gave the situation in the country the status of formal war.

Systematic political rape was intended not only to target girls and women but above all to affect their fathers or partners (or both) who were implicated in the resistance movements supporting Aristide's return (Merlet 2002, 164). Indeed, in most cases, the women had not committed any crime other than being the spouse or sister of a political activist (Bell 2001; Hamilton Phelan 1994; Kennedy and Williams 1995). Because girls and women were considered socially to be the property of men within the household as well as in the public domain, their bodies became "legitimate booty" and a "battle-camp trophy" for enemies (Bartlett and Rhode, 2006, 803; Brownmiller 1975, 32). The following two stories are typical (United Nations Social and Economic Council 2000, 15):

> On the night of 16 October 1991, Immacula was at home with her husband and six children, when a number of masked men with heavy weapons broke through the fence and invaded her home. The men put Immacula on the floor, handcuffed her husband, and then three of them raped her, hit her in the face and brutalized her in front of her husband and children. The youngest child, who is now six years old, still repeats the story of what happened that night. Because her husband supported Aristide, they were put into prison for six months, after which the family had to live in hiding. Once, when Immacula and her family were temporarily staying with her sister-in-law, her persecutors followed her into the house, raped her again and also raped her sister-in-law. Her sister-in-law died as a result of injuries sustained in the brutal rape, and Immacula has since had to take care of her sister-in-law's children as well as of her own.

> Saintanie's husband was a militant fighter for democracy. On 23 September 1993, his name was mentioned in a radio broadcast, along with those of other militant pro-democracy activists. That night, six masked men in black clothes forced their way into their house; three of the men took her husband with them and three of them raped Saintanie. Her six children were beaten with guns. After the incident, Saintanie and her children could no longer stay in their

house but fled to another neighborhood. They went to a refuge for Aristide supporters where they were given medical and psychological help as well as some financial assistance for a new place to live. Saintanie still feels victimized every day[.] . . . Her husband never returned.

Political rape often degenerated into the abhorrent variant of "forced rapes," in which men were induced, under threat, to rape their own daughters, sisters, or mothers in front of other relatives (Merlet 2002, 164). A professor of sociology at the University of Port-au-Prince reported in an interview that women also were forced to rape their own sons in front of other children in order to disband revolutionary groups and suppress their protests.

Further atrocities included psychological and physical torture of the victims, such as menacing them and raping them by using the barrels of guns or other bruising objects (Magloire 2004, 75). Several girls and women were shot inside their vaginas or died from the injuries inflicted by the brutal rapes; others still today face memories and the emotional and physical consequences of their traumatic experiences. A nurse who provided medical assistance to such victims gave the following account: "Women suffered enormously in the three years following the coup d'état. They [the military and paramilitary] raped them, they stuffed rifles up their vaginas and shot them, and pregnant women were beaten by the *chèf seksyon* [sheriff] until they aborted the children in their wombs" (Maternowska 2006, 66).

At that time, most of the victims were so traumatized and terrified of reprisals that they decided not to report the aggression to competent authorities. Representatives of the Human Rights Section of MINUSTAH, interviewed for the purpose of this research, reported the later testimonies of survivors of political rapes committed during the military coup. For example, they told the following story:

Yvette's boyfriend was a militant fighter for democracy. [One] night, six armed, masked men forced their way into Yvette's home. They killed her boyfriend, beat and kicked Yvette in the stomach with their army boots, and finally raped her before the eyes of her two sons, three and six years old. Yvette was seven months pregnant.

One week later, she had contractions and heavy bleeding. Despite the efforts of the doctor, Yvette's baby was born dead. . . . After the assault she also contracted sexually transmitted diseases and suffered from recurrent hallucinations. At that time, Yvette did not report the case because she was threatened with being killed. . . . Almost fifteen years later she finally told her story.   *Stats . . .*

Because of these dreadful manifestations of political rape and pressure, Haitian girls have continued to endure what the Special Rapporteur referred to as structural violence, which targets them as the most vulnerable people in society (United Nations Social and Economic Council 2000). Nowadays, political violence against girls, including that by the *zenglendos*, is still a common and punitive practice among rival political groups as well as a tool for terrorizing the entire population and controlling territory.

Studies have also highlighted the clear correlation between the use of violence against girls as a political weapon and the phenomenon of domestic abuse, revealing a proportional incidence between the two, the similar acts of violence employed, and the same degree of cruelty (Merlet 2002, 164). Gender inequality and sexual abuse perpetrated behind closed doors affect girls and women similarly in the public setting, where sexual assault becomes not simply a random crime, but rather a deliberate weapon of political and social oppression.

Gang Rape

In a country torn by poverty, political instability, inequality, and internal tensions, the widespread and systematic rape of women and girls has now become not only a political weapon of rival groups but also a common practice of criminal gangs implicated in illicit activities and aimed at controlling deprived communities. Informants of this study from MINUSTAH contended that in Haiti identifying and distinguishing different groups and objectives is a difficult task because their political strategies and social interests often blur with criminal and narco-trafficking activities.

Since Aristide's return to the government in 1994, the much-anticipated democratic consolidation has been undermined by deep conflicts among former allies; this situation ultimately produced political and economic stalemate. Internal discord and contradictions within the democratic party transformed important parts of urban popular organizations into violent government enforcers and criminal gangs struggling for control of metropolitan slums and for state favor. Given the numerous migrations from rural areas to Port-au-Prince and the poverty trap awaiting immigrants in the urban *bidonvilles* (shantytowns on the outskirts of cities) as well as the lack of state institutions and stability, the pool of potential recruits for criminal and political violence continues to grow.

In the slum areas of the capital, including Cité Soleil and Carrefour Feuille, where armed gangs dispute territory and violence and public disorder escalate to the point that even the PNH and MINUSTAH forces do not have access, girls, sometimes as young as four years old, suffer from widespread and systematic gang rape as a weapon of war and reprisal among rival groups. According to the UNICEF representatives interviewed, in the conflict areas of Port-au-Prince an estimated 50 percent of girls have been victims of rape, in most cases by more than one perpetrator. A *Lancet* survey in August 2006 showed that, during the twenty-two months of the interim government following Aristide's ouster in 2004, an estimated nineteen thousand women and girls were sexually assaulted in Port-au-Prince, primarily by criminals and political armed groups (Kolbe and Hutson 2006).

Representatives of the Ministry for the Status of Women, interviewed for the purpose of this study, revealed that to date no national aggregate data on sexual violence against girls and women are available. However, some NGOs and institutions, working on issues of sexual violence against girls in the conflict areas, individually keep records of victims and aggressive attacks. Informants from GHESKIO reported that, from 2000 to 2006, 3 percent of the victims were girls under ten years of age, and 73 percent were girls between ten and eighteen; 39 percent were virgins before the assault; 49 percent were sexually assaulted by more than one assailant, and 35 percent by seven assailants.

Gang rapes often resemble the practices of the *zenglendos* even though such violence is not always motivated by political purposes: the assaults occur in the evening or late at night; the criminals, who are armed and in groups of between three and twelve, break into the houses of the victims, beating and raping them one after another; the assailants sometimes abduct or kill the men of the family leaving the victims to fend for themselves, and often they return with more threats and intimidation. Informants from GHESKIO reported the testimony of Carline, a fifteen-year-old girl, who asked for their medical assistance after being sexually assaulted:

> [One] night while Carline was sleeping, five armed men burst into her home, threatening the entire family and attacking her father. While two of the men were burglarizing the house, the other three forced Carline to lie down on the floor raping her one after the other. Since the assault, Carline has never been able to sleep at night or leave her room during the day; she does not want to eat and is obsessed with flashbacks. Carline does not believe in the future any longer.

In the realm of social disorder and widespread violence in Port-au-Prince's shantytowns, women are also victims of gang rape in the middle of the street before the eyes of terrorized spectators or tacit accomplices. Participants in the Child Protection Unit of MINUSTAH reported to me the experience of Marie, a sixteen-year-old girl who was assaulted sexually in the slum of Carrefour:

> Marie and her thirty-three-year-old sister went to visit a friend who had had a baby the same day. On the way back home, they met three armed men who shoved the girls into a secondary street. Marie was raped in the middle of the alley by two of the men, while her older sister was sexually assaulted by the other. None of the neighbors or passersby intervened for fear of reprisal or because they were affiliated with the same gang. The perpetrators were identified as members of a criminal armed group responsible for gang rapes and kidnappings in the area. Since the assaults, the victims have repeatedly been threatened with death in the event that they report the assaults or even seek medical assistance.

Activists of KOFAVIV, a national NGO providing medical assistance to victims of sexual violence, revealed that criminals intentionally target virgins as a punitive measure and also because they are presumably not infected with HIV/AIDS. As a result, most of the victims assisted by the organization who are infected with HIV contracted the virus through rape (Fort 2006).

The following story exemplifies the brutality of gang rape (Panos-Caraibes 2007, 15):

> Claire is twenty-two years old. Her mother died, and since her father resides in France, she has been living in Port-au-Prince with her aunt and cousins for over ten years. The hosting family lives in the district of Canapé Vert, where Claire is used to walk[ing] around. One evening, around 7 P.M., she decided to go to the supermarket to do some shopping. On her way, Claire was approached by a group of four men, apparently friendly, who offered to walk with her. She just had . . . time to refuse when the group attacked her and dragged her into a dark alley. During that night, the four men raped Claire one after the other. She was so brutalized that she could not even scream. When they were satisfied, they ripped off her clothes, emptied her bag, and left her in the midst of the garbage. A pedestrian found her naked and bleeding. The following morning, Claire was taken immediately to GHESKIO medical centre, where she discovered, incredibly, that she had been infected [with] HIV.

Informants from MSF added that several times gang rapists have put sharp metal objects and bullets underneath their penis skin to assault girls; such objects provoke long-lasting hemorrhaging and other effects and permanently damage the girls' childbearing ability. According to the Lancet survey of August 2006, over 90 percent of sexual assaults committed by gangs in Port-au-Prince involved penetration of the victim's mouth, anus, or vagina with the perpetrator's genitalia or other bruising instruments (Kolbe and Hutson 2006, 5). The remainder of sexual assaults were sexual touching and the forced observation of sexual acts.

As was the case during the bloody military regime, the current outbreak of armed violence in the slums of Port-au-Prince and the copious violations of human rights are reminiscent of the features of a formal conflict. In the game of war, the social role of women's bodies as the property and appendage of men translates into their symbolic assimilation with the territory and collective spirit of an entire community. Keepers of the family honor and providers of the moral basis of a group's system, Haitian

Women used as a bargaining chip or property, not seen as full human beings [handwritten annotation]

girls and women become specific targets of gang rapes and armed violence perpetrated by rival factions as a weapon of destruction, submission, and humiliation. Sexual assault and violence not only are intended to reduce female bodies to "damaged property" (Brownmiller 1994, 92) but also ultimately are important tools for achieving the breakdown of the intimate structure of Haitian families and communities.

Representatives of the MINUSTAH Human Rights Section who participated in this study reported that in 2007 about sixty families living in the Cité Soleil slum lost their daughters because they either died of premature pregnancies or were murdered by the leaders of contending armed groups. Indeed, gang leaders often measure their power by their own women and resolve to kill them if they become the partners or concubines of their opponents. During the interview, one of the representatives of the Human Rights Section gave the following account:

> If a gang leader or one of his subordinates wants a girl to be his concubine, he can forcibly take her away from her family house. The parents of the girls are obliged to accept the fact that their daughter will sleep outside the home at night. If they refuse, they will be threatened with death, forced to leave the area and never contact their daughter again. If the girl refuses to follow the gang and to become the concubine of the chief or one of his subordinates, she will be gang raped by the entire armed group.

In contrast to the old myth that rape is a sexual expression of the male instinct, modern studies contend that "rape is not an aggressive manifestation of sexuality, but rather a sexual manifestation of aggression" (Seifert 1994, 92). Perpetrators' actions do not have much to do either with impulsive sexual desire or with a violent lack of self-control but rather with the deliberate resolve to dominate and deprecate the virtue and value of female bodies. Studies of the victims' perceptions indicate that their experience relates more to the feeling of submission and the invasion of physical and emotional boundaries than to their bodies' sexual subjugation. Even the perpetrators rarely experience sexual satisfaction but rather perceive an intense sensation of power, dominance, self-confidence, and virility.

Particularly in the case of gang rape, manliness and preeminence among the members of the group are the prevailing motivations for sexual violence against women. The conquest of the female body becomes a vehicle for extolling rapists' strength and masculinity as well as for displaying their status and authority within the gang (Magloire 2004, 74). In accordance with other research studies conducted in very different contexts (Sanday Reeves 1990), participants in this research also confirmed that rapes are often executed by the Haitian adolescents affiliated with vagabond gangs using a specific procedure: the order of choosing victims and the entitlement to do so is based on a gang member's rank and power in the group.

Interlocutors from the Ministry of Justice emphasized that "machismo is a transversal phenomenon" in the young and poor as well as the more mature and rich in Haitian society. Within such a setting, collective sexual violence becomes an exercise in virility, aimed more at developing bonds among men than on sexual contacts with women (Magloire 2004, 73). "Serial rape involves each successive male penetrating and ejaculating where another man has just done the same, a pattern of inter-male intimacy . . . which psycho-analysis proposes as primarily a sexual relationship between the men themselves" (Littlewood 1997, 14). Detached from images of women, rapists rarely remember their victims after the assault, as if the object of violence was not an individual but only a conceptual personification of a piece of unworthy property (Seifert 1994, 92).

Contemporary theories explain the different incidence of rape within various societies as the result of several variables (Porter 1986). A low rate of sexual assaults seems to occur in contexts in which male supremacy or strong female positions are assured, whereas societies characterized by uncertainty in the male social role and female subordination report a higher incidence of rapes. In Haiti, strong patriarchal values, cultural patterns of a power imbalance between men and women, and gender-specific sexual asymmetry are further exacerbated by poverty, poor governance, and armed violence, which ultimately foster the widespread and systematic rape of girls and women.

The above analysis regarding practices of sexual violence affecting women and girls in Haiti has revealed that gender disparity, patriarchal burdens, and abuse inside the household are the source of gender-based violence perpetrated in the public sphere as well. The following chapter focuses on the incentives and motivations that Haitian victims have to engage in retaliatory actions within the armed groups. The empirical findings presented accommodate women's and girls' narratives about the decision-making processes that lead to self-defense and revenge.

3

Understanding Women's Violence in Haiti

It is conventional wisdom that women are less violent than men in conflict settings. This view draws on biological evidence and on the way in which women are socialized beginning at an early age. Various scholars have, therefore, explained women's aversion to violence by emphasizing either their social role or their childhood socialization.[1] Consequently, when girls and women engage in violence, their antagonist behavior has usually been compared to that of their male peers, and it is often minimized by such a comparison or at least put into perspective by reason of the specific social, cultural, and economic circumstances associated with the notion of gender.[2]

In armed conflicts, this traditional view has critical consequences for women's agency. Several authors have emphasized that confining females to their biological fate as mothers and custodians of the private realm ultimately excludes them not only from the decision-making processes of war but also from peacemaking settlements and postconflict reconstruction (Puechguirbal 2004, 4–6; Tickner 1992). Either because of their nature or because they have been socialized to be good mothers and wives, women have been cast in subordinate roles in both war and peace. As Cynthia Enloe once claimed, "Militarized masculinity is a model of masculinity that is especially likely to be imagined as requiring a feminine complement that excludes women from full and assertive participation in postwar public life" (Enloe 2002, 23).

Empirical studies aimed at gaining insights into female combatants' participation in Northern Ireland, Sri Lanka, Colombia, and the

Philippines have revealed that girls and women are often as violent as, or even more violent than, their male comrades in seeking to find a way to assert their social status in highly patriarchal contexts (Alison 2004; Keairns 2002, 3–4). Similarly, a report commissioned by the Gender Unit of MINUSTAH and the UNDP (United Nations Stabilization Mission in Haiti and United Nations Development Programme in Haiti 2006, 17) on the situation of women in the context of armed violence in Haiti documents females' active involvement in armed groups as well as their ruthless actions.

The traditional view of women's peacefulness not only fails to provide a fair representation of reality but also ignores the incentives, conditions, and decision-making processes that motivate women to become active agents of aggression (Lombroso and Ferraro 1985; Pollak 1950). As a result, antagonistic feminine attitudes were interpreted as identification with masculinity (see Freud, [1905] 1953, [1925] 1961, [1931] 1961, [1933] 1964), contrary to the general rule that women tend to internalize their aggressiveness, whereas men are prone to externalize it (Hall 1978; Maccoby and Jacklin 1974). Only in the mid-1970s, after feminist theories began to question the social and cultural stereotypes that form the basis of gender inequality, did a more complex analysis of women and violence begin to appear in the relevant literature.[3]

Informed by such feminist discourses, more recent research has finally proposed a deeper rendering of females' active involvement in violence; this research contributes to an increased understanding of the motives and conditions that might foster or determine their decision making. Hence, empirical studies have increasingly begun to focus on females both within gangs responsible for community violence in inner cities (Fagan and Wilkinson 1998; Ness 2004; Sikes 1998) and within nonstate actors in contemporary conflict settings (Alison 2004; Sharlah 1999; West 2000). In particular, some of literature focuses on how girls and women are often coercively drawn into civil wars to serve as combatants and agents of aggression (Cairns 1996).

In another trend, the current literature has investigated the reasons why females join armed groups voluntarily and become combatants within their ranks. Scholars have argued that women are often moved by ideological goals and, thus, are more likely to join factions that seem to pursue revolutionary goals and social-change strategies, as in the case of the Irish Republican Army in Northern Ireland (Alison 2004). Political aims have also inspired the resistance of female combatants who have served the rebel forces in South Africa, Palestine, and several Central African conflicts (Baker 1991; West 2000).

Participants in these studies have revealed a vast range of justifications for engaging in violent actions. Some reported having deliberately chosen to join the armies, and, thus, they did not see themselves as victims of war or as members of vulnerable groups but rather as those who had espoused the revolutionary cause (Gibbs 1994). For instance, a study conducted with female ex-combatants in the guerrilla army Frelimo during the Mozambique independence war between 1964 and 1974 revealed that those women had purposely joined the conflict to contribute to the social construction of new gender roles and identities within the revolutionary movement and the quest for a free country (West 2000). Finally, other research on African civil conflicts has found that women join the rebels as fighters in exchange for food, shelter, security, and companionship (Boyden 1994; Keairns 2002, 3–4).

Other scholars have explored the relationship between sexual harm and female criminality. Some have explained girls' and women's rationale for aggression and delinquent behavior as a healing response to the long-lasting consequences of prior sexual abuse and injury (Runtz and Briere 1986; Schaffner 2006). Studies conducted in the US juvenile legal system estimated that over 90 percent of girls in custody had previous experience with physical, sexual, or emotional abuse (Acoca and Dedel 1998). A nationwide survey conducted by the American Correctional Association of girls detained in juvenile correctional facilities revealed that over 54 percent of them had been sexually abused and 61 percent had been physically abused (American Correctional Association 1990). Drawing on such empirical results, researchers have further linked girls' and women's involvement in assaults and conflicts to their need to protect themselves or to the anger resulting from the sexual and physical injury they have previously experienced (Wolfe and Tucker 1998).

To comprehend the connection between female victimization and retaliation, the current literature has properly broadened to include a focus on the surrounding context of girls' and women's lives (Schaffner *good phrase*

2007, 1230). Empirical evidence suggests that women's experiences of cumulative victimization, intertwined with loss and penury, race and gender inequality, social ostracism and stigmatization, dramatically influence and restrict their choices of livelihood, safety, coping mechanisms, and methods of survival (Wesely 2006). Particularly in warlike situations, it has been acknowledged that "violence becomes normalized, even utilized, as an emotional strategy and a psychological response to troubles and frustrations" (Wesely 2006, 1243; see also Scheper-Hughes 1992).

So far in Haiti, current research has focused primarily on gaining perspective on the patterns of risk factors for the widespread and systematic sexual violence affecting girls and women. Indeed, besides carrying out a few studies addressing female participation in aggression—studies that have been promoted by international organizations operating in the country and conducted in partnership with civil society organizations—scholars still have not explicitly treated the nexus between sexual violence against girls and women and their active involvement in armed violence. By combining empirical evidence with pertinent theories applied in similar contexts, this chapter presents evidence from Haiti on female participation in the armed groups as well as on the victimization-offending nexus. In particular, the following discussion examines the conditions, rationale, and decision-making processes that persuade Haitian women and girls to engage in violence. This chapter thus fills a gap in the current literature on female aggression and its interplay with previous sexual victimization.

Women's Participation in Armed Violence

According to the accounts of international organizations operating in Haiti that have been corroborated by empirical evidence collected in this research, women and girls in Haiti not only are victims of armed violence but often join the armed factions either as partners and concubines of gang members or as ruthless perpetrators; they actively participate in illicit activities such as kidnapping, extortion, and narco-trafficking as well as in violent attacks against the local population or rival groups. Although precise figures on female participation in the gangs are not available, data collected in the three major urban settings most affected by armed violence—Port-au-Prince, Gonaives, and Cap-Haitien—revealed that girls and women are generally associated with the majority of the armed groups except for the political ones.

As noted earlier, the sexual division of labor in Haiti prevents women from engaging in political life. Gender hierarchies define specific roles and impose a separation of tasks between men and women. Haitian women are socially and culturally expected to be solely responsible for the household, taking care of children and doing domestic chores. Scholars have stressed that, since the formation of the Haitian state, women have been considered second-class citizens; they achieved political rights only in the 1950s and are still struggling to obtain full citizenship (Magloire 2004; Merlet 2010). Not surprisingly, therefore, none of the politically motivated armed groups in Haiti has a female leader or members. Although women are excluded from the political organizations, they still support their men and partners who actively participate in the groups. In the hope of improving their families' living conditions, women comfort their men, who are members of these organizations, as caring mothers, wives, or sisters but never engage in executive activities as autonomous participants.

In contrast to the conclusions drawn by other studies conducted in a variety of conflict settings, such as in South Africa, Palestine, and several Central African conflicts (Baker 1991; West 2000), these findings reveal that female participation in armed factions is not politically motivated in Haiti. Therefore, theories that women's rationale for violence is their pursuit of ideological goals and social change are not applicable in the Haitian context. This conclusion contrasts with the evidence of high male adhesion to the political organizations in Haiti. The findings demonstrate that, unlike men, women living in poor communities are minimally engaged in either public or political actions, and their lack of involvement reinforces the gender disparities in lower Haitian society.

Another, practical reason for women's exclusion from the political organizations is that members of these groups typically use large-caliber weapons, such as the Galil and MI4s and MIs (Puechguirbal, Man, and Loutis 2009). Such weapons are considered to be "male tools" and, thus, are not appropriate for women to use. While men always utilize large-caliber weapons, women usually employ different arms according to the type of armed group that they join.

Although identifying and distinguishing different armed groups in Haiti is a difficult task because their structures, strategies, and purposes often change as a result of changes in their criminal interests and in political and social developments, the factions that recruit girls and women as perpetrators of violence can be placed in the following main categories: *milices populaires* (popular organizations), armed criminal gangs, and Brigades de Vigilance (vigilante groups).[4]

The popular organizations comprise young Haitians and former police personnel and security forces. Their aim is to control the impoverished areas of the capital by targeting the local population. These groups function as local militias whose goal is to cleanse the Port-au-Prince *bidonvilles* of rival gangs. Former policemen who are now members of the popular organizations provide the groups with weapons and free access to the slums. During their raids, the popular organizations may target all individuals regardless of whether they are acquaintances, neighbors, or related to their rivals and regardless of who is hiding and sheltering them. In practice, these organizations hold entire communities collectively accountable for the wrongdoings of the opposing armed groups.

The popular organizations are also involved in illicit activities, such as kidnapping, extortion, and trafficking in drugs and arms. Girls and women are actively engaged in these groups, pursuing their goals, fighting alongside men, and attacking civilians in the violent confrontations. They are armed with batons and machetes, whereas male members utilize both small- and large-caliber weapons. Women are often used by the groups to lure potential targets of kidnapping, to facilitate their capture, and to hide hostages in their houses.

Similarly committed to organized crime are the armed criminal gangs. Oppressive poverty, high unemployment rates, and poor governance in the last few decades have resulted in the breakdown of slum communities, leading to the emergence of these criminal groups. Engaged in various illicit activities, such as kidnapping, trafficking in drugs and arms, as well as in violent armed confrontations against opposing factions, these groups target girls and women for gang rape, abduction, and sexual slavery as a means of controlling the community and spreading terror among the civilians. Women members of these groups become active agents of violence, kidnapping, and other criminal activities. They often act as informants and are armed with small-caliber weapons.

Some armed criminal gangs comprise solely female members and are believed to be responsible for sexual violence against their hostages or members of rival groups. In Port-au-Prince, the three main armed groups composed solely of women are Fanm Boss (female bosses), Fanm Pye Poro (women with green feet), and Baz Madivin (a group composed exclusively of lesbians) (Puechguirbal, Man, and Loutis 2009). (The name Fanm Pye Poro is apparently derived from the green color of US dollars, which is the currency usually requested for ransoms.) Fanm Boss and Fanm Pye Poro have been responsible for kidnapping operations. Baz Madivin collaborates with male gangs by coordinating kidnapping operations, transferring hostages, and collectively raping them.

Opponents of the popular organizations and the armed criminal gangs are the Brigades de Vigilance, aggressive self-defense associations that comprise teenagers and adults of both sexes; they were formed in response to the escalating violence and criminality in the slum communities. The primary goal of these organizations is to protect their families, homes, and personal values from firearm attacks by bandits, gangsters, robbers, and rapists.

To fight assailants, female participants in the vigilante groups usually employ *armes de jet* (thrown weapons), including conch shells, stones, and glass bottles, and *armes blanches* (batons), such as daggers and machetes. Women also mobilize to organize solely female vigilante groups that operate in defense of a specific area. In Gonaives, there are two main vigilante groups that comprise only women: Lame Boutey (army using glass bottles) and Lame Polanbi (army using conch shells). These neighboring rival armed groups employ glass bottles and conch shells, respectively, during their confrontations.

Women's Violence: Survival Strategy or Deliberate Choice?

The majority of women interviewed for the purpose of this study as well as those participating in the focus-group sessions openly discussed their wretched living conditions and the oppressive poverty and insecurity affecting their neighborhoods. When asked to describe the areas they live in, their stories closely resembled one another. Despite their different ages, backgrounds, and life histories, none of the women seemed to be able to cope with the grievous difficulties of their lives. Furthermore, they did not appear to be able to imagine any alternative other than leaving their areas and moving to wealthier neighborhoods of the capital. One young girl vividly portrayed the slum where she lives in Port-au-Prince as follows: "It is very poor, crowded with desperate people looking for food and hope. Actually, they have lost all their hope and they are just angry, desperate, and waiting to die. I just cannot stand it anymore. . . . The houses are crap, dirty and dark . . . but I was born there, and I am used to it, you know."

When asked whether they feel safe in their neighborhoods, women lamented the dangers engulfing their streets and the gangs who rob their houses, terrorize their children, and dispose of their bodies as their own property. Their reflections also suggested the intimate correlation between indigence, violence, and human decay. An interviewee gave the following account: "Safe? Oh no, [I do] not [feel safe] at all. . . . Poverty and violence come together, you know. . . . The armed groups control the area: they can do whatever they want. They were born there and know everybody and own everybody. That's what they think at least, and what all the people think. They enter the houses, rob, rape, and threaten. And people just don't know what to do; . . . they just don't know what to do." Many times, as soon as the discussion focused on the incentives women who have been daily victims of terror and violence might have to become actively involved with their own assailants in the gangs, some participants became speechless, suggesting their remoteness from the armed factions. Others honestly contended that "it is impossible not to get involved with the armed groups when your children are starving and you just eat once a day if you are lucky." In other words, in the impoverished slum communities that are ignored by the police, gangs bring food and money together with terror and war, forcing civilians to fulfill their own needs and blurring the line between unforgivable violence and survival strategies.

Representatives of AVSI, an international NGO working to provide education and other services in one of the areas most affected by armed violence in Port-au-Prince, recalled the words of a girl serving a gang by spying on police movements and carrying arms: "My family was killed and my brother starved to death; now I eat and, one day, the chief will send me to school and pay my fees." In a place without law, order, and human compassion, gangs distribute the ransom from kidnappings and the proceeds from narco-trafficking and other criminal activities among the population, providing food and basic resources and even paying the funeral expenses for those who die. Poverty and desperation are intertwined in the lives of both victims and perpetrators, who often switch roles. "My rapists were killed by a rival group in a gunfight. In the end, everybody needs to pay," a victim asserted. Another explained the repugnance she felt seeing her assailants every day and having to meet their demands: "I have a friend who is blind, and she was raped like me, but now she cannot recognize her assailants. Sometimes, I wish I could be her and not have to cross the street and bump into them or work for them to get some money. I wish I could be her because my sight does not bring me any good."

In general, most women justified their active involvement in the armed groups as being the result of their unbearable poverty and the lack of other resources to support their children and families. A few of them disagreed, countering that serving the gangs is ultimately a deliberate choice, a convenient solution; thus, they suggested that even in extreme poverty, degradation, and distress, individuals can still exercise free will and good judgment. When asked whether, in her opinion, women join the bandits because they are poor and desperate, a young rape victim dissented, stating: "No, I think that they made a choice. I know a lot of other people who are poor, and I am kind of poor too, but I did not end up in a gang. Yeah, being poor sucks, but you can't go around robbing the others or raping girls and making war in the streets before the eyes of children."

Other informants also expressed controversial opinions on this topic. A representative of the Ministry for the Status of Women declared that "not all the poor become bandits. Therefore, it is a life choice to join the armed groups." On the contrary, a professor of sociology at the University of Port-au-Prince claimed that some women are obliged to join the gangs because of contingent circumstances. In fact, they are so poor that they feel unable to leave the slums controlled by the armed groups and, thus, end up serving them out of fear of retaliation. Another professor in the Psychology Department of the University of Port-au-Prince argued that some girls are taken prisoner by the gangs during their raids and are then forced to associate with the groups. Other women, however, lured by promises of money, food, or other benefits, may have made a choice to follow the armed groups.

Reasons for Female Participation in Armed Violence

The above excerpts from the interviews and focus-group sessions reveal the complexity of rape victims' lives, which are torn apart by cumulative victimization and the everyday struggle against hunger, insecurity, and degradation, and thus they confirm that a contextual approach is essential to comprehending female violence in Haiti. The following sections of this chapter investigate some of the reasons for girls' and women's participation in armed violence. Drawn from interviewees' responses and focus-group discussions, this analysis contributes to evaluating whether and to what extent women's violence should be understood as a survival strategy, a direct response to sexual harm previously experienced, or a deliberate choice to retaliate.

Need for Protection

A study conducted by the Gender Unit of MINUSTAH and the UNDP (United Nations Stabilization Mission in Haiti and United Nations Development Programme in Haiti 2006) on the situation of women within the context of armed violence reported a strong female component in the ranks of the vigilante groups. In Gonaives, two of the vigilante groups, Lame Boutey and Lame Polanbi, include only female members within their ranks.

The interviews and focus-group discussions substantially confirmed such data and the intrinsic characteristics of these armed segments. Women of different ages openly confessed to having been involved with militant self-defense groups at some point in their lives, fighting bandits and rapists within their neighborhoods. They lamented the escalation of violence and criminality swamping their communities and putting their children's lives and their own at risk.

Some women revealed that they had been solicited to join the vigilante groups by their own men, who were already members of the militant organizations. Others, being widows or heads of the household, mentioned the daily challenge of defending their children from the same violence that they had experienced. Despite disparities in age, background, and family history, all the women declared that their sole motivation for joining the vigilante groups was the urgent need for protection and self-defense. When asked what they thought about responding to violence with further violence, one woman simply countered: "You know, nobody really cared when my husband was murdered and I was beaten and raped until I fainted. Why should I care now about the others? I just want to protect my babies. . . . I just want my daughter not to have to suffer what I suffered."

Representatives of the Ministry for the Status of Women who participated in this study confirmed that women's need to survive within a militarized space, such as the slums controlled by the armed groups, inevitably conditions their demand for protection. In particular, in the shantytown of Bel Air, in Port-au-Prince, women who are heads of their households because they have been abandoned by their husbands or partners agree to become sexual slaves of the gangs in exchange for their protection.

Along the same lines as the MINUSTAH-UNDP study above, interviews with other experts in the field provided consistent descriptions of the armed confrontations. Serving on the frontline immediately behind the child soldiers, women use primarily batons, daggers, and machetes, rather than firearms, to fight against bandits and rival groups.

When I investigated why women decided to adopt aggressive strategies of self-defense rather than resorting to police intervention, participants in the study unanimously revealed their total distrust of the security system. They confirmed that for a long time police did not even have access to the conflict areas in Port-au-Prince, Gonaives, and Cap-Haitien. Moreover, women deplored both the futility of police intervention and the often corrupt relationships between the wrongdoers and security forces. Some of them even revealed that asking the police for help might put them in further danger. Excerpts from an interview describe the views of a young woman on this issue:

INTERVIEWER: What about the police? Do the police intervene?

INTERVIEWEE: Ah, the police . . . better not to even see them. The police are scared; they did not even have access to the area until a few months ago. . . . And if they are not scared, they can be even worse than the bandits. You call the police for help, and they can rape you as well. There is no difference . . . no difference at all.

INTERVIEWER: No difference between what?

INTERVIEWEE: No difference between the police and the gangs. They all have guns and they can do whatever they want. You just cannot do anything against them.

A representative of a civil society organization responsible for the psychological recovery of rape victims reported the story of a girl who asked a policeman for help while she was being gang raped by three armed men. The police officer simply joined the assailants in raping the girl. Furthermore, a patient assisted by a center providing medical care for rape survivors recounted having been beaten, raped, and sodomized for several hours by a police officer and his accomplices. Medical exams attested to the fact that the assailants had lacerated the woman's genitals from the vagina to the anus before abandoning her in the street. Similar instances were recalled by participants in the focus-group discussions. Hence, the majority of women avowed that, feeling unsafe in their own homes and being aware of or having personally experienced police corruption and abuse, they had resolved to become members of the vigilante groups as a result of their primary need to protect their families and themselves.

A professor in the Sociology Department of the University of Port-au-Prince, interviewed for the purpose of this study, reported the story of a vigilante group in Bel Air comprised solely of female members.

Native women of Bel Air decided to organize a Brigade de Vigilance to protect their neighborhood from the armed groups. They were outraged that other women, who were not from Bel Air but had arrived there as spouses or concubines of the gangs' members, were taking over their territory. Initially, the native women of Bel Air even tried to call the police and let them into the neighborhood hoping that they would chase the gangs away. However, when the police entered the slum, they attacked indiscriminately the entire community, assuming that even civilians were either associated with or supporters of the armed groups. The population of Bel Air then huddled around the gangs. In response to such a failure, the native women of Bel Air decided to stick together and create a Brigade de Vigilance. They confronted the women affiliated with the armed groups both with *armes de jet,* including conch shells, stones, glass bottles, batons, and *armes blanches,* such as daggers and machetes. In the end, they managed to originate a revolt of all women from Bel Air against their foreign rivals.

The professor concluded by saying that order was soon and easily reestablished in the area by the gangs using firearms. His account exemplifies the escalation of violence that traps women living in the slums either way—as ruthless members of the armed groups or as victims responding to violence with more violence in order to protect their identity, families, and territory.

Anger

Poverty, despair, and the lack of state intervention fuel the discontent of slum inhabitants. Some of the interviewees and focus-group participants expressed their resentment for the dearth of financial aid and consideration received from the government. They bemoaned the immense social inequality that divides the country into a few wealthy castes, on the one hand, and the hopeless masses, on the other. In their complaints about their unprivileged condition, women often recalled the sorrowful legacy of colonialism. In particular, they blamed the dark color of their skin compared to the lighter shades of the middle class, and the slave origin of their clans that is still imbued in current generations.

Disparities and oppressive poverty are also believed to be the basis for the kidnapping waves that have plagued the cities of Port-au-Prince, Gonaives, and Cap-Haitien. A professor of sociology at the University of Port-au-Prince, interviewed for the purpose of this study, provided political reasoning for the escalation of kidnapping. He recalled that Aristide had given the poor hope for a better future. But by blaming the bourgeoisie, he further nurtured the original conflicts within Haitian society. After Aristide's ouster from the country in 2004, indigent communities, living in the shantytowns of the main cities, revolted against the subsequent administration and demanded his return. Since then, the government has failed to provide prompt and adequate responses to the social exclusion and the lack of education, employment, and access to basic services of the poor communities, which, as a result, have become increasingly marginalized, angry, and resentful.

Since 2004, many women associated with either the popular organizations or with the armed criminal gangs have played key roles in kidnapping operations by identifying, shadowing, and luring the targets. In some cases, women have deceptively approached potential targets while they were driving, asked for a ride, and then taken them to meet their kidnappers. They generally employ small-caliber weapons to conduct their lucrative activities (Puechguirbal, Man, and Loutis 2009). Looking less suspicious than men, women often carry ransom money or weapons from one base of the armed groups to another and also watch and report the movements of the security forces. Finally, they are usually responsible for feeding and hiding hostages in their houses.

None of the women participating in this study actually admitted to having been involved in a kidnapping operation. However, they were still able to provide relevant insights into the potential motivations behind such behavior. In their extended narratives, anger was the most recurrent incentive for retaliation. Deprived of their basic entitlements and the ability to have a tolerable existence, women directed their resentment toward the state and the society. A middle-aged woman explained: "Women are victims of everything, and we, raped victims, are even more so. But we don't get anything from the state, not even a place in the society . . . not even food, money, or respect. Why should we respect the society then? I just want to tell you something . . . if people don't receive what they are entitled to, people will take it anyway by themselves. . . . This is what is happening. This is what all violence and kidnapping are about." Representatives of the MINUSTAH Gender Unit confirmed that rape victims struggle to find food, money, and work. Conscious of their social needs and basic rights, they then deliberately retaliate against the society and the official institutions that are neglecting them.

When asked whether such motives could justify the kidnapping of children, a participant claimed: "When women are so desperate they just remember to be their own children's mothers. They would do anything for them." A representative of the MINUSTAH DDR Unit who agreed to participate in this study explained that the armed groups have strategically targeted children in their kidnapping operations to demonstrate the failure of the current government to protect the population. By recruiting women, who socially represent the custodians of the private realm, to actively conduct these operations, the armed groups have engendered the breakdown of morals and the intimate structure of Haitian families and communities.

Women living in poor communities are consumed by rancor and jealousy and feel powerless in the face of social inequities, failing institutions, and an inert government. They often end up venting their anger against each other, to the point that they become instigators or agents of cruel crimes. As one young interviewee explained:

> The first time I was [raped I was] sixteen years old. I remember that I was walking alone in the street. . . . I met these three guys and they told me that they wanted to talk to me. I knew they were in the gangs; . . . also they had guns and I was sure that they wanted to threaten me when they pulled me over and asked me to follow them. . . . They told me that someone had paid them to kidnap me and then kill me. And I asked them who this person was who wanted to kill me. I said, "I am a nice person and I don't bother anybody, and how come someone wants to kill me?" They told me that they could not tell me who this person was, but that it was the truth. . . . [Then] they gave me an option. . . . I could choose between being killed or raped. I don't remember what I replied. I couldn't breathe. I just recall that they started beating me and two of them raped me one after the other. . . . I cannot be sure who was the person that paid them, but there was this woman who was a neighbor [and who] did not like my mom, and I think she wanted to punish her. . . . She was envious that my mom had opened a business, like a store, and got most of her clients. . . . She wanted to punish her because she knows that my mom loves me so much.

A professor in the Sociology Department of the University of Port-au-Prince reported that some women out of greed and resentment urge their husbands or partners to participate in kidnapping operations against other women. In particular, he gave the following account based on a research investigation conducted in Bel Air:

Women in Bel Air are so jealous of one another. First, they want to show that they are more powerful and richer than the female members of the gangs who are not originally from Bel Air but had moved into the area with the armed groups as concubines of the chief or his subordinates. Second, they also compete with their peers, who are native women of Bel Air. The only way women believe they can win such competitions is by showing their wealth. Therefore, they become envious of the other women's houses, clothes, and possessions. They are so angry at the society and their own communities that they feel entitled to extort money from them. Therefore, women force their husbands to organize or participate in kidnapping operations. In the case of refusal, they take over the leadership of the groups and conduct the operations themselves.

Revenge

The data suggest that while older women tended to resort to violence and criminal activities primarily because of their need for protection or their resentment at being deluded and forsaken, younger women revealed an additional motivation behind their decisions to participate in armed violence. During focus-group discussions, they condemned the restrictive social expectations that confine them to preserving the domestic realm and, above all, pressure them to marry. In their accounts, a marriage presents the sole opportunity women have to escape a future of indigence and misery. Given their wretched living conditions, girls, not surprisingly, seemed to value a relationship with a man much more for its material and economic return than for affection and companionship. In practice, if economic potential is perceived as a screening device for men, virginity is definitely the necessary requirement for women to be marriageable.

Interviewees and participants in the focus-group sessions openly shared their anxiety about this issue, acknowledging that their status as rape victims had permanently ruined any opportunity they might have to get married and, therefore, any hope for a better future as well. Girls also lamented the cruelty of their own communities, which marginalize them for their misfortune and mock their grief. When asked whether after being gang raped she had received any help or support from her community and neighbors, a young woman replied:

Never! They are so awful and mean to me. You know, my community is making fun of me because I am a rape victim. That's what I am, that's the only thing I am to them. . . . I have no place in the society, no future, and nobody will marry me this way. When I was raped . . . and I lost my virginity, I wanted to die rather than being marginalized by my own community. I have never had a boyfriend, you know, . . . and I am twenty-seven years old. I would love to forget everything, but people are so cruel that they make me remember everything when I see a sarcastic smile on their face. The worst thing of this entire story is the blame of the society. I have been blamed as if I was responsible for what happened to me and I deserved it.

Given their stigmatized status and lack of economic prospects, some girls suggested that joining the armed criminal gangs was the only alternative left. Marginalized by their community and often abandoned even by their own families, these girls found a new social identity and a source of economic support in the outlaw organizations.

A psychologist working for the NGO GHESKIO, providing medical assistance to rape victims in Port-au-Prince, confirmed that many girls are rejected by their own families after an attack. She explained that some of them who are extremely traumatized and vulnerable react to such violent experiences by identifying with their assailants. In need of protection, they eventually end up building a relationship with them and joining the gangs. During another interview, the GHESKIO psychologist recounted the experience of one of her patients who, after being expelled by her family, decided to join the gang whose members had brutally raped her because she found a form of affiliation with the group that she had lost with her own family and community.

Becoming members of the armed groups or spouses and concubines of their adherents provides girls with the basic necessities of life, such as food, clothing, shelter, and, above all, with the leverage to regain the regard of their own communities and thus to vindicate their reputation. A representative of an international NGO working for a vocational program designed for girls currently detained in the female prison of Port-au-Prince confirmed that most of the inmates have been accused of the offense of association with armed groups. He also explained that the main incentive young women have to become involved with the gangs is their pressing need to gain social respect, nourish their self-esteem, and ultimately avenge their injuries. *So much damage done to get revenge for*

The head nun at a religious institution based in the slum of Cité Soleil in Port-au-Prince, which provides shelter, food, schooling, and vocational education to girls living in the area, most of whom have been sexually abused, gave the following account during our encounter:

> Rose was of one my girls, and she had come to our school since she was little. A couple of years ago, I noticed that she was not coming to school on Fridays. When I asked her the reason, she replied that her mom was working and she had to look after her younger siblings. After a few days, I began to see some changes in her behavior. She was wearing new and expensive clothes, a little jewelry and sunglasses. Her classmates came to tell me that Rose had a new and rich boyfriend. She was only thirteen years old, and I was concerned what kind of guy this could be. I then discovered that Rose was the girlfriend of Evans, the chief of the armed group Boston, responsible for so much violence, kidnapping, and trafficking in Cité Soleil. I also found out that on Fridays, when Rose was not coming to school, she was helping and participating in such illicit activities. . . . One day, I called her into my office to confront her. She told me proudly that Evans had chosen her because she was prettier than the other girls. And now, she was pregnant and, somehow, conscious that she did not have any better option than staying with him and his gang. She had food there and things that she could have never afforded before. "It's not that bad to be his woman," she told me. Indeed, even if she was pregnant, the other girls respected and feared her because she was the woman of the boss, after all. . . . In vain, I tried to persuade her to end this relationship and come to live with us for a while. A few days after our meeting, she stopped coming to school for good. I have never seen her again. Only a month later, I heard that Evans was arrested.

In addition, the head nun claimed that, in the Haitian slums, some girls are raped and then forced to join the armed groups, but many others, like Rose, feel somehow honored and proud to be chosen by the leader of a gang or his subordinates to become part of the group. The girls need money and are more attracted by nice clothes and expensive objects than by the prospect of an honest life. To be sure, some families reject their daughters once they have lost their virginity, but others boast of their girls to their community and often benefit from their new financial status. *More reasons for them to continue*

Similar accounts were offered by the head priest responsible for another religious organization operating in Cité Soleil that provides shelter and vocational education to children and girls associated with the armed groups as well as to young prostitutes. He confirmed that girls are often forced to join the gangs and become concubines of their members because they fear retaliation against themselves and their families. However, in many cases, lacking food, work, and money to pay their school fees or hospital bills, they choose to affiliate with the armed groups in the hope of better prospects. Especially for girls who became prostitutes after their assault, joining a gang is the only opportunity they see to redeem themselves in the eyes of their community and to regain social status.

When the leader of a gang has enough money to burn US dollar bills in front of people or to organize the shipping of a truck full of rice to distribute to the applauding crowd, it is difficult for young girls to resist the temptation of becoming his concubine or a member of his group. Sexually abused, gang raped, or trapped in the circle of prostitution, they rarely see a better option for their future than joining the criminal gangs and regaining a respectful status within their community.

The analysis above has provided a general understanding of women's violence based on a review of the relevant literature. Furthermore, empirical evidence from Haiti, collected during the fieldwork for this study, has been used to assess the incentives and motivations that Haitian women have to join the armed groups and to become perpetrators of violence. In particular, the three major factors that encourage women and girls to engage in criminal and community violence are their need to protect themselves and their families, their resentment toward state negligence and denial of their plight, and their dysfunctional desire to attain personal and social respect through retaliation. The next chapter provides the international legal framework for addressing gender-based violence and women's violence as well as the Haitian legal measures currently in place regarding the protection of women and girls and their accountability for associating with armed groups.

They're hated for being assaulted + losing virginity so they see no choice but to regain respect and status by far

4

Legal Frameworks

This chapter examines the international legal norms addressing practices of discrimination and sexual violence against women under international human rights and humanitarian law. It discusses the shortcomings of these laws in responding to such violations and effectively protecting women and girls. The chapter also examines UN resolutions on women, peace, and security that develop, at a programmatic level, women's participation in postconflict processes and reconciliation. Finally, the Haitian legal framework on gender-based violence and women's involvement in armed violence is analyzed in its progression from the original Haitian penal code to the current laws in compliance with international benchmarks.

Gender-Based Violence under International Law

Women's rights under international law fall primarily into two different categories of provisions: nondiscriminatory norms, providing equal treatment for women and men, and protective measures from gender-based violence (Charlesworth and Chinkin 2000, 213). Because Haiti has ratified the main international treaties dealing with women and children, the Haitian criminal justice system should refer to and sustain these human rights benchmarks in responding to practices of discrimination and sexual violence against women and girls in the country.

The Charter of the United Nations, signed on June 26, 1945, was the first international agreement recognizing the equal rights of men and women and including as a purpose of the United Nations itself the promotion and encouragement of respect for human rights and for fundamental freedoms for all without any distinction based on sex.[1] Along the same lines, in 1948 the General Assembly of the United Nations adopted the Universal Declaration of Human Rights, proclaiming that all human beings are born free and equal in dignity and rights without any distinction based on gender (arts. 1 and 2). The intrinsic value of any individual life as well as the right to equal treatment and nondiscrimination on the basis of sex have been specific objects of protection under international law not only through generally applicable provisions but also through women-specific instruments, which have been ratified by, among others, the Haitian government.

After receiving general acknowledgment of these protections, women's organizations advocated for the establishment of specific mechanisms aimed at advancing women's status in the international arena and raising awareness of the necessity for their protection. During the fortunate decade of 1975–1985, women's activism gained momentum by promoting studies on women's issues and, most important, by lobbying for the adoption of the Convention on the Elimination of All Forms of Discrimination Against Women (CEDAW), the first international instrument espousing gender equality as its sole focus and acknowledging women as victims of unique human-rights violations.

Adopted in 1979 by the General Assembly, the CEDAW defined the term *discrimination against women* to encompass any distinction, exclusion, or restriction made on the basis of sex that has the effect or purpose of impairing or nullifying the recognition, enjoyment, or exercise by women of human rights and fundamental freedoms (art. 1). Moreover, States Parties[2] to the CEDAW, among which Haiti has been included since July 20, 1981, committed themselves to condemning discrimination against women in all its forms and agreed to adopt all the appropriate measures, including legislation, to modify or abolish existing laws, customs, and social and cultural patterns of conduct held by men and women, with a view to achieving the elimination of prejudices, whether customary or not, that

VERY present in Haiti

are based on the idea of the inferiority or the superiority of either of the sexes or on stereotypical roles for men and women (arts. 2 and 5).

In order to achieve the CEDAW's stated goals, Article 17 established a Committee on the Elimination of Discrimination against Women (the CEDAW Committee), a supervisory body responsible for monitoring members' efforts to meet their obligations through a review of periodic reports submitted for consideration by States Parties (arts. 17–21). Comprising independent experts elected by States Parties for their high moral standing and specific competence in the field, the CEDAW Committee also has the task of turning the process of revising reports into a constructive dialogue on crucial women's issues as well as drafting compelling general recommendations and providing valuable insights for women's international conferences (Byrnes 1995).

At the Final Conference, held in Nairobi, Kenya, at the end of the UN Decade for Women in 1985, activists for women's rights reached a breakthrough consensus stating that "[violence against women] exists in various forms in everyday life in all societies. Women are beaten, mutilated, burned, sexually abused, and raped. Such violence is a major obstacle to the achievement of peace and other objectives of the Decade and should be given special attention. . . . National machinery should be established in order to deal with the question of violence against women within the family and society" (United Nations 1986, para. 258, as cited in Thomas and Beasley 1993). Besides informing the international debate, world conferences and in-depth studies on women's issues have been a significant source of knowledge for the CEDAW Committee as well, helping to ensure a dynamic interpretation of the Convention over time.

The promulgation of general recommendations became an important tool for interpreting the Convention on issues extending beyond the discrimination framework as well as for ensuring its punctual application to serious violations against women (Byrnes 1995). Although the general recommendations are not legally binding in the same way as the CEDAW, they clarify States Parties' obligations when they are not mentioned or adequately explained in the text. In the case of violence against women, for instance, the silence of the Convention was subsequently replaced by two general recommendations on the topic. The first one, General

Recommendation No. 12, issued by the monitoring body in 1989, acknowledged States Parties' obligation to protect women against violence of any kind occurring within the family or in any other area of social life and to include in their periodic reports to the CEDAW Committee legislation in force and statistics regarding gender violence.[3]

The second recommendation, General Recommendation No. 19, promulgated in January 1992, developed the issue further, asserting that the broad definition of discrimination against women also includes any practice of gender-based violence—that is, violence directed against a woman because she is a woman—or any practice that affects women disproportionately.[4] It pointed out that cultural norms that regard women as inferior to men and that make them victims of social stereotypes perpetuate a structure of subordination and generate patterns of gender-based violence that ultimately impair or nullify women's enjoyment of human rights and fundamental freedoms. Furthermore, acknowledging the fact that wars often lead to increased prostitution, sexual assault, and trafficking in women, General Recommendation No. 19 called on member states to devise specific protective and punitive measures (art. 16).

Only at the end of the twentieth century were women's legal entitlements fully vested via the recognition of women's rights as human rights. This concept is based on an understanding of equality that extends beyond *de jure* equality as prescribed by the norm of nondiscrimination to ensure to women throughout their lives the same choices, respect, and integrity, and the same understanding of human dignity, as is accorded to men. An effective interpretation of equality between men and women should, in fact, encompass the following definition: "Gender equality means an equal visibility, empowerment, and participation of both sexes in all spheres of public and private life. Gender equality is the opposite of gender inequality, not of gender difference, and aims to promote the full participation of women and men in society" (Council of Europe 2004, 8).

Thus gender equality means ensuring women's empowerment through the recognition of their full legal and civic status as well as their participation in both the public and the private spheres. It also involves state and individual responsibility for the violation of women's human rights and for gender-specific violations of human-rights law, such as violence against women, whether committed by state or nonstate actors in armed conflict or nonconflict situations.

The assertion of women's rights as human rights was historically made at the World Conference on Human Rights, held in Vienna in 1993, and was further reiterated in the Beijing Platform for Action, agreed to at the Fourth World Conference on Women in 1995. Indeed, at the 1993 World Conference on Human Rights, the CEDAW Committee, concerned about the fact that some groups of women, among them female children and women in the midst of armed conflict, are especially vulnerable to violence, fostered the adoption of the Declaration on the Elimination of Violence against Women by the UN General Assembly.[5]

The Declaration defined violence against women as any act of gender-based violence that results in, or is likely to result in, physical, sexual, or psychological harm or suffering to women, including threats of such acts, coercion, or arbitrary deprivation of liberty, whether occurring in public or in private life (art. 1). The terms of the Declaration specifically include in the category of violence against women any physical, sexual, and psychological violence occurring in the family, including battering, the sexual abuse of female children in the household, dowry-related violence, marital rape, female genital mutilation, and other traditional practices harmful to women (art. 2(a)).

One of the most significant endeavors of the international community to eradicate violence affecting women worldwide, the Declaration also encouraged data collection and the compilation of statistics concerning intimate abuse and the prevalence of different forms of violence against women. Its most significant legacy has been studies on the causes, nature, gravity, and consequences of abuse against women as well as the evaluation of the effectiveness of measures and strategies implemented to prevent and redress violence against women (art. 4).

In addition to the adoption of the Declaration, a further outcome of the 1993 World Conference on Human Rights was the 1994 appointment of Radhika Coomaraswamy as the first Special Rapporteur on violence against women, including its causes and consequences, by the Commission on Human Rights.[6] Aimed at creating an institutional mechanism for regular in-depth study and reporting on violence against women worldwide, the mandate included recommendations regarding potential strategies and practical measures to eradicate violence against women and its causes as well as adequate remedies for its consequences.

Through engaged analysis, specific recommendations, and targeted country visits, the Special Rapporteur has worked to raise awareness of the matter within the international human-rights community as well as in local contexts, contributing to an increased understanding of the relevant international standards. In Coomaraswamy's words, the violence-against-women movement has been "perhaps the greatest success story of international mobilization around a specific human rights issue, leading to the articulation of international norms and standards and the formulation of international programs and policies" (Coomaraswamy 2005).

The categorization of violence against women as a human-rights issue has important and critical consequences. Acknowledging violence against women as a violation of human rights conveys binding obligations on States Parties to prevent, eliminate, and prosecute practices of abuse against women and holds states accountable if they fail to comply with such commitments. Thus, claims on States Parties to take all appropriate measures to combat inequality and to protect and promote human rights for women shift from the sphere of discretion and become, on the one hand, legal entitlements for citizens and, on the other, obligations of states.

The concept of state responsibility has traditionally been understood under international law on human-rights violations as arising only when acts of violence against women can be imputed to a state or any of its agents. Because sexual abuse and rape usually involve private individuals, sexual-violence crimes have long been deemed outside the scope of state accountability. However, the concept of state responsibility has been expanded to include not only state actions but also their omissions and failure to take appropriate measures to protect and promote women's rights.

Accordingly, in addition to refraining from committing violence against women through their own agents, states must also fulfill the obligation to prevent human-rights violations by private individuals by investigating relevant allegations, prosecuting the perpetrators, and providing adequate remedies for victims. States can therefore be held accountable for violence against women because "although the state does not actually

the State's

commit the primary abuse, ~~its~~ failure to prosecute the abuse amounts to complicity in it" (Thomas and Beasley 1993, 41).

In theory, then, states have a duty to protect women from violence and can be held accountable if they fail to do so. The standard of due diligence required has been articulated in General Recommendation No. 19: States Parties "may also be responsible for private acts if they fail to act with due diligence to prevent violations of rights or to investigate and punish acts of violence, and for providing compensation." States' liability, therefore, should be construed on a case-by-case basis, through the criteria of reasonableness, based on the general principles of nondiscrimination and good faith. Yet, the standard of due diligence requires States Parties to use any appropriate measures at their disposal to address both individual acts of violence against women and structural causes so as to prevent future violations and to punish wrongdoers.

Further procedures to enhance state accountability for violence against women are contained in the Optional Protocol to the Convention on the Elimination of All Forms of Discrimination against Women.[7] In force since December 22, 2000, the Optional Protocol includes a complaints procedure enabling individuals to petition for rights or to complain about violations of rights and also an inquiry procedure allowing the CEDAW Committee to conduct inquiries into serious and systematic abuses of women's human rights occurring within the States Parties to the Optional Protocol.

Under the complaints procedure the CEDAW Committee is able to focus on individual cases and to develop jurisprudence for any specific matter. Through the inquiry procedure, the CEDAW Committee can investigate substantial abuses in which individual communications and complaints have failed, address a broad range of critical issues in a particular country, and release specific recommendations on the structural causes of violence. To date 187 countries, including Haiti, as mentioned above, have either ratified or acceded to the CEDAW, meaning that over 90 percent of the members of the United Nations have agreed to it. However, only 104 countries, not including Haiti, have assented to be parties to the Optional Protocol and to be bound by its improved and additional enforcement mechanisms for women's human rights.

The lack of a judicial enforcement mechanism to enact the CEDAW provisions implies that the primary tool of compliance is the judiciaries of the States Parties. Legal systems vary significantly in recasting the universal principles provided in international agreements into domestic legal formulations. The common-law tradition, for instance, requires the adoption of a specific statutory law by the competent legislative body in order to bind a state to the terms of an international agreement. Legal systems within the civil-law tradition, like Haiti, provide for the self-execution and immediate enforceability of international provisions but still require an internal legislative effort to craft such principles into domestic law.

On the regional level of the inter-American human rights system in Latin America, the 1994 Inter-American Convention on the Prevention, Punishment, and Eradication of Violence against Women (hereinafter the Convention of Belém do Pará) adopted by the OAS in 1994, sets forth binding obligations for thirty-two States Parties, among them Haiti, which was goaded to ratify the convention by the national organization Mouvement des Femmes Haitiennes (Haitian Women's Movement) on April 3, 1996 (Magloire 2004, 70).[8] States Parties to the Convention of Belém do Pará declare that violence against women shall be understood to include physical, sexual, and psychological violence perpetrated or condoned by the state or its agents regardless of where it occurs. Furthermore, the Convention of Belém do Pará acknowledges that violence against women is an offense against human dignity and a manifestation of the historically unequal power relationships between women and men (Preamble and art. 2).

Specifically for girls, the Convention on the Rights of the Child of 1989, ratified by Haiti on June 8, 1995, prohibits discrimination against children on the basis of their gender and provides that States Parties shall take all appropriate legislative, administrative, social, and educational measures to protect children from all forms of physical or mental violence, injury or abuse, neglect or maltreatment, including any form of sexual abuse and exploitation (arts. 2, 19, and 34).[9] In addition, States Parties ensure that no child is subjected to torture or other cruel, inhuman, or degrading treatment or punishment (art. 37(a)). Particularly in situations of armed conflict and violence, States Parties should respect and guarantee compliance with rules of international humanitarian law applicable to them in armed conflicts that are relevant to the child and should take all feasible measures to ensure the protection and care of children who are affected by armed conflicts (art. 38).

Commitments undertaken by the members of the World Conference on Women in Beijing in 1995 include the determination to ensure the full enjoyment by girls of all human rights and fundamental freedoms and to take effective action against their violation and failure to protect them by repealing existing laws and regulations as well as by removing discriminatory customs and practices affecting girls. Moreover, members of the 1995 World Conference on Women acknowledged that the maintenance of peace and security at the global, regional, and local levels, together with the prevention of policies of aggression and ethnic cleansing and the resolution of armed conflict, are crucial for the protection of the human rights of women and girls as well as for the elimination of all forms of violence against them and of their use as a weapon of war.

Although Haiti is party to both the CEDAW and the Convention on the Rights of the Child, informants to this study working for the Gender Unit of MINUSTAH deplored the fact that since the UN Special Rapporteur on Violence against Women visited Haiti in 1999 violence against girls and women continues to occur on a structural level. Concerns and reproaches from the international community remain unanswered and largely ignored, and recommendations aimed at eradicating discrimination and violence against girls and women in the country have not been effectively implemented.

Given the difficult condition of children and the widespread and systematic perpetration of sexual violence against girls in the country, the UN Special Representative of the Secretary-General for Children and Armed Conflict, for the first time, included Haiti among the countries listed in the report of the Secretary-General on children and armed conflict to the Security Council in 2006 (United Nations General Assembly/Security Council 2006). As a general principle, Security Council Resolution 1539 of April 22, 2004, strongly condemns, among other practices, "rape and other sexual violence mostly committed against girls . . . as well as forms of slavery and all other violations and abuses committed against children affected by armed conflict."[10]

Although the dynamics of violence in Haiti are different from those in other countries, paragraph 96 of the Secretary-General's report on children and armed conflict to the Security Council dated 2005 expressly provides that "there is no universally applicable definition of armed conflict . . . and the Special Representative of the Secretary-General for Children and Armed Conflict has adopted a pragmatic and cooperative approach to this issue, focusing on ensuring broad and effective protection for children exposed to situations of concern, rather than on the definition of the term armed conflict" (United Nations General Assembly/Security Council 2005).

Specifically regarding gender, Resolution 1325 on Women, Peace, and Security, adopted by the Security Council in 2000, asserts the important role of women in the prevention and resolution of conflicts and in peace-building operations as well as the need to fully implement international humanitarian and human-rights laws protecting women's rights during and after conflicts.[11] Along the same line, the United Nations Security Council Resolutions 1743, 1780, and 1840, extending the mandate of MINUSTAH, strongly condemn the widespread rape and other sexual abuse of girls in Haiti and reaffirm MINUSTAH's policy of promoting and protecting women's rights as well as of reckoning with gender considerations as a cross-cutting issue throughout its mandate.[12]

Gender-Based Violence and Women's Violence under International Humanitarian Law

The primary area of international law addressing women and girls either as victims or as perpetrators of violence in hostilities is international humanitarian law. The Xth Hague Convention (the Hague Convention) and the Geneva Convention for the Relief of the Wounded and Sick in Armies in the Field (the First Geneva Convention), of 1907 and 1929 respectively, were the first two legal instruments under international humanitarian law aimed at protecting women's human rights in conflict.

Indeed, the Hague Convention began to protect women victimized by armed conflict violations providing that "family honor and rights . . . must be respected" (art. 46). Serving as the mainstay of the family reputation, women were intentionally targeted by indiscriminate rapes, abductions, and murders committed as weapons of terror and intimidation of entire communities. Subsequently, the First Geneva Convention provided that women who had been wounded or had fallen sick while fighting in the battlefield should be treated with all consideration due to their sex (art. 12).

Further provisions for women combatants were included in the 1929 Geneva Convention relative to the Treatment of Prisoners of War (hereinafter the 1929 Geneva Convention), setting forth that prisoners of war were entitled to respect for their persons and honor. In particular, due to the specific risks faced by women because of their gender, the 1929 Geneva Convention included a protective measure for women combatants requiring that women shall be treated with all consideration due to their sex. It also stated that any difference in the treatment of the prisoners of war shall be prohibited except on limited grounds, among which the "sex of those who benefit from" such distinctions (art. 4). Finally, the 1929 Geneva Convention included specific protective measures aimed at deterring gender-based violence and the degrading treatment of female prisoners by requiring mandatory separate accommodations and conveniences for men and women in the camps (arts. 25 and 29); prohibiting punishment of women that was harsher than that inflicted on men for a similar offense (art. 88); and finally providing that the disciplinary punishment of female prisoners should be executed under the immediate supervision of women (art. 97).

With the adoption in 1949 of the Geneva Convention Relative to the Protection of Civilian Persons in Time of War international law for the first time extended protection to women and children as members of the civilian population. The much-anticipated provision set forth that women should be especially protected against any attack on their honor, in particular against rape, enforced prostitution, or any form of indecent assault (art. 27). Under the terms of the 1949 Geneva Convention, States Parties undertake to enact any legislation necessary to provide effective penal sanctions for persons committing, or ordering to be committed, any of the "grave breaches" listed in the Convention itself, among which rape, enforced prostitution, and sexual assault are not explicitly mentioned (art. 146). As a last resort, a broad interpretation of the term *grave breaches*, including acts "willfully causing great suffering or serious injury to body or health" (art. 147), may be extended further to also embrace violations of women's rights and sexual integrity (Chinkin 1994; Meron 1993). Nevertheless, the loose formulation contained in the 1949 Geneva Convention impeded the effective prosecution of such crimes.

The flaws of the 1949 Geneva Convention were partially remedied in 1977 by the adoption of two additional protocols.[13] Explicitly intended to update the provisions contained in the previous Conventions, Protocol I (regarding the protection of victims of international armed conflict) and Protocol II (regarding the protection of victims of noninternational armed conflict) included protective provisions for both women and children. In particular, Protocol I required that women be given special respect and be protected in particular against rape, forced prostitution, and any other form of indecent assault (art. 75). Protocol II equally prohibited outrages upon personal dignity, in particular humiliating and degrading treatment, rape, forced prostitution, and any form of indecent assault (art. 4). In terms of prosecution, Protocol I included within grave breaches "inhuman and degrading practices involving outrages upon personal dignity, based on racial discrimination" (art. 85) but did not classify as grave breaches discriminatory practices based on sex.

As for children, although the two protocols did not explicitly provide for gender-related distinctions, they generally prohibited the participation of children under fifteen years of age in hostilities. In particular, Protocol I called on parties to a conflict to take all feasible measures to ensure that children below the age of fifteen do not take a direct part in hostilities (art. 77). This formulation raised the critical question of what should and should not be interpreted as direct participation and the reasons for such a distinction.

As a matter of fact, modern conflicts have increasingly recruited and used children in many different ways. This is particularly the case for girls, whose involvement in armed forces may range from acting as cooks and porters of weapons to messengers and combatants, thus leaving unsettled the issue of whether these various roles fall within the purview of the provision. Protocol II attempted to remedy this flaw by clarifying that children under fifteen years of age should neither be recruited by armed forces or groups nor be allowed to participate in hostilities (art. 4).

More recently, the 1998 Rome Statute establishing the International Criminal Court listed within crimes against humanity rape, sexual slavery, enforced prostitution, forced pregnancy, enforced sterilization, or any other form of sexual violence of comparable gravity committed against civilians in conflict settings (art. 7). Furthermore, it provided that recruiting children under the age of fifteen into the national armed forces or using them to participate actively in hostilities is a war crime—a serious violation of the laws and customs of international armed conflict (art. 8).

Similarly, the Convention on the Rights of the Child set forth that member states should take all feasible measures to ensure that children under the age of fifteen do not take a direct part in hostilities (art. 38). Once again, such a provision leaves open the legal issue of how to protect those children, many of whom are girls, who are involved in the conflict but perform duties apart from serving on the battlefield. Despite the fact that the Optional Protocol on the Involvement of Children in Armed Conflict, adopted by the United Nations General Assembly in 2000, increased the recruitment threshold to eighteen years of age, it did not solve the "direct-participation" question.[14] Rather, it further provided a controversial disparity between state armed forces, which are required to take all feasible measures to ensure that children under eighteen do not take a direct part in hostilities (art. 1), and nonstate actors, which should not, under any circumstances, recruit persons under the age of eighteen in hostilities (art. 4). Arguably, this set of asymmetrical obligations might easily lead to noncompliance by member states and parties to the conflict.

Women, Peace, and Security

Worldwide, violence against women has been committed and widely tolerated in wartime. Only in the 1990s, after the massive sexual assaults reported during the Yugoslavian conflict, did rape finally begin to be recognized and prosecuted as a human rights violation per se. In the midst of the Yugoslavian conflict, an estimated twenty thousand to fifty thousand women suffered from rape and other sexual atrocities (Bartlett and Rhode 2006, 805).

The UN Security Council acknowledged such practices as "massive, organised, and systematic," aimed at intimidating, degrading, and terrifying an entire ethnic group.[15] From 1991 to 1994, in Croatia and

Bosnia-Herzegovina, Serbian soldiers captured thousands of women, imprisoned them in concentration camps, and engaged them night after night as sexual slaves. Most victims were forcibly impregnated, intentionally refused abortions, and obliged to procreate Serbian babies according to a specific genocidal strategy aimed at creating a dominant ethnicity and eradicating the others. An anonymous victim from Bosnia recounted: "They liked to punish us. They wanted women to have children to stigmatize us forever. The child is the reminder of what happened" (United Nations Population Fund 1999, 12). *Access to women's bodies is so political*

Similarly, in the Rwandan conflict, rape was employed as a tool of genocide. In only four months, from April to July 1994, Hutu soldiers attempted to destroy the population of Tutsi, committing mass rapes against an estimated 250,000 to 535,000 Tutsi women. One of the Hutu leaders, Laurent Semanza, abetted the perpetration of such violations by saying, "Are you sure you are not killing Tutsi women and girls before sleeping with them? . . . You should do that and even if they have some illness, you should do it with sticks" (quoted in MacKinnon 2006, 220). Testimonies recount that "not a single Tutsi woman or girl who remain[ed] alive from the conflagration was not sexually assaulted. Rape was the rule and its absence the exception" (quoted in MacKinnon 2006, 220).

The intense media coverage of women raped to death or lethally mutilated horrified the international community. Widespread and systematic violations affecting women in both conflicts were documented in such detail and so vividly transmitted worldwide that an urgent demand for an international legal response was created. In 1993, the UN Secretary-General established an ad hoc tribunal, the International Criminal Tribunal for the Former Yugoslavia, to prosecute the war crimes committed.

Likewise, one year later, the outbreak of violence and human-rights outrages in Rwanda led the Security Council to establish the International Criminal Tribunal for Rwanda. Indictments of both ad hoc tribunals for the first time acknowledged and led to the prosecution of mass rape as a legitimate crime against humanity and a tool of genocide against unwanted groups; one of the indictments declared that "the systematic rape of women . . . is in some cases intended to transmit a new ethnic identity to the child. In other cases humiliation and terror serve to dismember the group."[16]

After the indictments by the Yugoslavian and Rwandan international tribunals, the Fourth World Conference on Women, held in Beijing in 1995, identified women and armed conflict as one of the most critical areas of concern. Delegates solicited "governments, the international community and civil society, including non-governmental organizations and the private sector . . . to take strategic action" in relation to "the effects of armed or other kinds of conflict on women" (Gardam and Charlesworth 2000, 149–150). They also called for upholding and reinforcing the norms of international humanitarian and human-rights law in relation to the offenses against women and their effective prosecution. But, above all, the Beijing Platform for Action, elaborated at the conference, avowed that "women play an important role as promoters of peace," and, therefore, their "full involvement in all efforts for the prevention and resolution of conflicts [is] essential for the maintenance and promotion of peace and security."[17]

The new trend inaugurated in Beijing enhanced international awareness of and debate about these issues. The commitments made in the Beijing Platform for Action culminated, a few years later, in the breakthrough UN Resolution 1325 on Women, Peace, and Security adopted by the Security Council on October 31, 2000 (see note 11 in this chapter). Resolution 1325 was the culmination of several decades of gradual realization of the diverse roles that women can play both in conflict and in peace making, and it was as well the outcome of feminist activism and advocacy by women's organizations. It combines in one document the general assumptions and programmatic recommendations common to international-law instruments with specific suggestions for practical intervention measures.

Inferences from universal international-law principles can be found throughout the text. The Preamble recaps the document's lineage from previous resolutions and the commitments of the Beijing Platform for Action as well as its direct inspiration in the "purposes and principles of the Charter of the United Nations and the primary responsibility of the Security Council . . . for the maintenance of international peace and security." Further references are made to the 1949 Geneva Convention, Protocols I and II, as well as to other international-law instruments applicable to the rights and protection of women and girls in armed conflicts. The language of Resolution 1325 itself recalls the programmatic terms of international-law documents "encouraging," "calling on," and "urging" either member states or the UN Secretary-General to take all appropriate actions for its effective implementation.

Resolution 1325 includes specific provisions for its concrete application. To begin, it reaffirms the important role of women in the prevention and resolution of conflicts and in peace-building and clearly states its ambit of interest. Consequently it emphasizes the importance of the equal participation and the full involvement of women in promoting and maintaining peace and security and in conflict prevention, management, and resolution at all decision-making levels. The call to fully implement international humanitarian laws and human-rights laws protecting women and girls during and after armed conflict is accompanied by various practical measures. They include mine-clearance and mine-awareness programs, gender mainstreaming in peacekeeping operations, specialized training in women's human rights for all peacekeepers, institutional arrangements for women's protection and full participation in peace making, and HIV/AIDS awareness training for member states' civilian and security personnel before their deployment on peacekeeping missions. Other primary objectives are increasing the presence of women in UN field-based operations; increasing the number of women in military and civilian humanitarian operations and strengthening their role and contributions to these efforts; and appointing more women as special representatives of the Secretary-General.

A key provision reinforcing the Resolution 1325 efforts to bridge the gap between international-law directives and grassroots initiatives is the requirement that Secretary-General missions consult local and international women's associations on gender concerns and rights. In addition, all actors involved in the negotiation of peace settlements are required to take into account women's needs during rehabilitation, reintegration, and postconflict reconstruction as well as to "support local women's peace initiatives and indigenous processes for conflict resolution." Even the wording of these operational provisions blends the Secretary-General and member states together with all parties to armed conflict as interlocutors of Resolution 1325; this blending reinforces the essential goal of converting institutional approaches into a constructive dialogue among all actors involved to create a cooperative strategy for peace making.

In content, Resolution 1325 replicates the findings of the ad hoc tribunals regarding violations affecting women in wartime. It "calls on all parties to armed conflict to take special measures to protect women and girls from gender-based violence, particularly rape and other forms of sexual abuse." Yet, it reiterates the responsibility of states to end the impunity toward genocide, crimes against humanity, and war crimes, including sexual offenses targeting women and girls in armed conflict; moreover, it emphasizes the need to prosecute these crimes despite any amnesty provisions. In line with the indictments of the two ad hoc tribunals, Resolution 1325 acknowledges warlike atrocities affecting women to be crimes against their right to integrity and security rather than as indecent assaults against their honor.

Moreover, Resolution 1325 provides that women can be not only victims but also actors in war: "all those involved in the planning for disarmament, demobilization, and reintegration [have] to consider the different needs of female and male ex-combatants and to take into account the needs of their dependents." Acknowledging women as potential perpetrators of violence themselves or even as only mothers, spouses, and daughters of ruthless soldiers creates new possibilities for them to become beneficiaries of rehabilitation programs and to attain a better future in society. Whether they are implicated in the dynamics of war or are simply civilian victims of violence (as are children), Resolution 1325 calls on women to play an active role at the negotiation table in devising peace agreements and plans for postconflict reconstruction.

The content of Resolution 1325 was complemented and expanded by the passage of UN Resolution 1820 and subsequently of UN Resolution 1888 and UN Resolution 1889 (all on women, peace, and security).[18] Resolution 1820 acknowledges that women and girls are particularly targeted by the use of sexual violence as a tactic of war to humiliate, dominate, instill fear in, disperse and/or forcibly relocate civilian members of a community or ethnic group. It further recognizes that sexual violence used as a tool of war can significantly exacerbate situations of armed conflict, may impede the restoration of international peace and security, and, in some instances, may persist after the cessation of hostilities. Given its condemnation of the use of rape and other forms of sexual violence in armed conflict, Resolution 1820 calls on member states to comply with their obligations to prosecute the perpetrators of sexual violence, to ensure that all victims of sexual violence have equal protection under the law and equal access to justice, and to end impunity for sexual violence.

Moreover, Resolution 1820 emphasizes that the persistent obstacles and challenges to women's participation and full involvement in the prevention and resolution of conflicts as a result of violence, intimidation, and discrimination erodes women's capacity and legitimacy to participate in postconflict public life. Acknowledging the negative impact the lack of women's involvement has on durable peace, security, and reconciliation, including postconflict peace-building, Resolution 1820 reaffirms the important role of women in the prevention and resolution of conflicts and in peace-building, in addition to the need to increase their active participation in decision making with regard to maintaining and promoting peace and security.

Resolutions 1888 and 1889 both complement Resolution 1820. In particular, Resolution 1888 requests the Secretary-General to rapidly deploy a team of experts when situations arise that are of particular concern regarding sexual violence. It further calls for the appointment of a Special Representative to lead efforts to end conflict-related sexual violence against women and children and to ensure that information about the prevalence of sexual violence is included in a report by UN peacekeeping missions to the Security Council. Resolution 1889 reaffirms the provisions of Resolution 1325, emphasizing the need for member states to effectively implement them. To ensure implementation, Resolution 1889 calls on the Secretary-General to develop a strategy, including appropriate training, to increase the number of women appointed to pursue good offices on behalf of the Secretary-General and to submit a set of indicators to track implementation of Resolution 1325 within six months.

National Legislation

The classification of sexual assaults and rape in the Haitian criminal-justice system has undergone several changes. Until 2005, according to article 279 of the Haitian Penal Code of 1835, which was based for the most part on the French Penal Code of 1810, anyone who committed a crime of rape or was responsible for any other assault on morals executed or attempted with violence against individuals of one sex or the other should be punished with detention. According to the following article, 280, if the crime was committed against a child under the age of fifteen, the perpetrator should be punished with imprisonment.

This initial taxonomy of rape among the *atteintes aux bonnes moeurs*—assaults on morals—reflected the common understanding that the harm inflicted by sexual violence consisted in a damage of the victim's honor and dignity rather than a crime against her physical integrity and well-being (Human Rights Watch and the National Coalition for Haitian Refugees 1994). The language of the Haitian criminal provisions revealed the patriarchal perception of girls and women's social role as keepers of the family honor and their responsibility for the community's moral system as well as the customary misconception of their bodies as men's property.

The Decret modifiant le régime des aggressions sexuelles et éliminant en la matière les discriminations contre la femme (Decree Changing the Regulation of Sexual Aggressions and Eliminating Forms of Discrimination against Woman), adopted in July 2005, recognized that the crime of rape required reinforcement of its sanction; acknowledged that the provisions under the Haitian Penal Code established practices of discrimination against women that contravened the precepts of the Haitian Constitution and the international commitments undertaken by the Republic of Haiti; and, finally, redefined rape as a criminal offense and a sexual aggression against the victim rather than a moral assault.

In a new section of the Haitian Penal Code entitled "Sexual Aggressions," the amended article 278 provides that anyone who commits a crime of rape or is responsible for any other type of sexual aggression executed or attempted with violence, threats, surprise, or psychological intimidation against an individual of one sex or the other should be punished with ten years of forced labor. The new version of the following article, 280, states that if the crime is committed against a child under the age of fifteen, the perpetrator shall be punished with fifteen years of forced labor.

Specifically for restavèks, the Loi relative à l'interdiction et à l'élimination de toutes formes d'abus, de violences, de mauvais traitements ou traitements inhumains contre les enfants (Statute Related to the Interdiction and the Elimination of All Forms of Abuse, Violence, Maltreatment, and Inhuman Treatment against Children), adopted on June 5, 2003, provides that the term *abuse and violence against children* refers to any form of maltreatment or inhuman treatment; thus, any practice of abuse and violence against children, including their sale, traffic, and employment for forced services and labor as well as their recruitment for sexual abuse and exploitation or their use as a weapon of war, is prohibited.

Informants from UNICEF and representatives of the Ministry of Justice interviewed for this study revealed that although significant amendments have been made to the Haitian Penal Code and important enactments have been adopted, in practice, little substantive change has occurred and the Haitian legal culture remains deeply imbued with its discriminatory and macho heritage. The legacy of social hierarchies and patriarchal values as well as the lack of capacity and resources in the security and justice services impede the pace of legal implementation and undermine the effective application of the law.

With respect to girls and women who are members of armed groups, article 225 of the Haitian Penal Code holds them generally accountable for the offense of association with malefactors. The crime of association with malefactors is inherent in the gang organization, including correspondence between the women and their leaders and agreements for the distribution and partition of illicit proceeds; the crime is punished with forced labor if it is not accompanied by other crimes (art. 226). If the members provide any service to the gangs or procure arms, munitions, or instruments of crimes, the punishment is imprisonment (art. 227). Records of the female prison in Port-au-Prince revealed that over 50 percent of inmates have committed the offense of association with malefactors, a statistic that reveals the high rate of female participation in armed violence in Haiti (data from my fieldwork/interviews).

By juxtaposing Haitian legislation with international legal norms, the analysis above has examined the expected Haitian compliance with international obligations and the Haitian legal responses to sexual violence against women and girls as well as to their subsequent involvement in violence.

This overview of the current legal framework is supplemented in the following chapter by descriptions of shortcomings in the relevant laws and of the severe impact gender bias has on the Haitian security and judicial systems; the result is a lack of effective prevention strategies and protection measures for human-rights violations against women and girls.

5

Victims' Help-Seeking and the Criminal-Justice Response

In spite of the commitments to the international community by the Haitian government and the efforts undertaken by the national legislature, sexual abuse and rape are still widely and systematically perpetrated throughout the country across social and economic lines. The underreporting of women' rights violations, the loss of rape cases at various stages of the criminal-justice process, and, ultimately, the widespread impunity with which males perpetuate sexual violence against women derive from the inequalities in the formal legal system, the victims' internalization of gender stereotypes and hierarchy, their fear of social stigmatization and reprisal, and the high levels of corruption and dysfunction within the security and judicial sectors.

During my fieldwork in Haiti, I interviewed many women who had been victims of sexual violence either in the domestic realm or in the context of armed violence. As explained in Chapter 3, some of the victims decided at some stage in their life to join the armed groups and become perpetrators of violence. Rape and sexual abuse are so pervasively perpetrated in Haiti that women and girls are often victims not only of incest or of the fury and revenge of gangs but even of random attacks by strangers and neighbors. Poor social conditions, domestic unrest, and rampant poverty afflict the majority of the Haitian population, of which women and girls remain the most vulnerable part. In most countries, sexual violence against women and girls is widely underreported. Haiti is no exception.

Indeed, when I interviewed representatives of civil society organizations providing medical assistance and psychological support to rape victims, they lamented their patients' reluctance to report the attacks to competent authorities. Some of these organizations were exploring the possibility of including judicial assistance in their services. However, they reported that when asked whether they wanted to press charges and pursue judicial proceedings, most women firmly refused.

Consistent with such accounts, among all the victims I personally interviewed for the purpose of my research, only one of them had reported the attack. She revealed having been raped twice, but only the first time did she report the crime to the authorities. Therefore, my recurrent question to representatives of civil society organizations was why women victims of sexual violence seek justice so seldom and why the outcome is so poor for the very few who do.

The following analysis aims to respond to such questions by providing insights into women's and girls' decision making around help-seeking and resistance. It provides a deep understanding of the cultural barriers and the practical and institutional obstacles Haitian women face when they are in need of protection and justice. In particular, the following sections investigate the shortage of police and prosecutorial systems, the lack of enforcement, and the ultimate implications these obstacles have on women's decisions about reporting cases of rape. No proper understanding of the shortcomings and failures of the criminal-justice responses to gender-based violence and women's violence in Haiti can be achieved without an engaged analysis of the different actors, functions, and responsibilities involved in the system.

Finally, this chapter also includes an analysis of a few more recent proceedings that have succeeded in providing judicial redress to the claimants. The aim is to discern the reasons for these few but nevertheless positive outcomes and the incentives women had to report the attacks in these cases, as well as to suggest improved ways of responding to violence against women.

Underreporting of Rape Cases

Representatives of the Ministry for the Status of Women interviewed for the purpose of this study asserted that the lack of official national statistics on violence against girls and women significantly limits an accurate evaluation of the situation in the country and, ultimately, compromises any attempt by women's associations and civil society institutions to raise awareness and promote the political legitimacy of the issue.

According to a study of 1,705 women undertaken by the Centre Haïtien de Recherches et d'Actions pour la Promotion Féminine (CHREPROF) (1996) and reported by the Special Rapporteur on violence against women on the mission to Haiti (United Nations Economic and Social Council 2000), an estimated 66 percent of victims (girls and women) never reported attacks for fear of reprisals and social ostracization, as well as because of the lack of adequate legal mechanisms and support structures.

More recently, representatives of MINUSTAH and national civil society organizations who were interviewed for this research confirmed that the majority of sexual abuses and rapes against girls and women are never reported to the police or other organizations. For example, in 2006 and 2007, only one rape case per year was successfully prosecuted.

Despite the dearth of reporting about human-rights violations against girls and women, the Commission de Collecte des Données (Commission for the Collection of Data) of the Table de Concertation Nationale sur les Violences Faites aux Femmes (National Round Table Consultation on Violence against Women) ascertained that from 2002 to 2005 the number of documented cases of sexual violence increased at a faster rate per year than cases of any other type of violence (Table de Concertation Nationale sur les Violences Faites aux Femmes 2005).[1] Yet, the Commission reported the following figures from the disaggregated data of the three major national organizations providing assistance to victims of sexual violence:

- At SOFA, the number of rape cases in 2005 was twelve times greater than in 2003
- At Kay Fanm, the number of rape cases almost tripled from 2003 to 2005.
- At GHESKIO, the number of rape cases in 2004 was 4.5 times greater than in 2002, and the number tripled in 2005.

According to SOFA, which provided the only data on victims' recourse to medical assistance and the judicial system from 2003 to 2005:

- In 2003, almost 8 percent of the victims sought medical assistance and visited the police subsequent to the attack.
- In 2004, 31 percent of the victims sought medical assistance, and 11 percent visited the police after the attack.
- In 2005, almost 19.4 percent of the victims sought medical assistance, whereas only 7.2 percent visited the police after being sexually assaulted.

More recently, an informant from Kay Fanm reported that, in 2006, 224 cases of violence against women were taken to the judicial system. Among those, 120 cases were dismissed before the judgment and, of the remaining 104 cases, only one ended in a conviction. Similarly, during the first half of 2007, Kay Fanm reported that at least 155 cases of violence against women were taken to court. Out of the forty-one rape cases—among which thirteen were perpetrated against young girls, twenty-one against teenagers, and seven against women—only one ended in a conviction.

The lack of reporting on human-rights violations against girls and women and the extent of the attrition of rape cases in the Haitian criminal-justice system result from a combination of several factors, including the victims' internalization of gender inequalities and stereotypes, fear of social stigmatization and reprisal, the corruption and dysfunction of the security and formal legal systems, and the exercise of discretionary power by criminal-justice personnel at various stages of the process. Whether because of discretion, reluctance, or complicity, the significant loss of rape cases from the criminal-justice system reveals a troubling pattern of incentives aimed at the recurrent denial of justice for victims of sexual violence and abuse.

Gender Stereotypes and Social Stigmatization

The internalization of customary norms that place men at the top of the gender hierarchy and women at the subservience level of families and communities was corroborated in all the victims' stories that were collected for this study. The common pattern of male dominance and female subordination experienced by female informants within Haitian households was embedded, on the one hand, in the social role of men as the providers and primary owners of the family assets and, on the other hand, in the women's duty to serve their spouses and to comply with their orders and will. The interviews revealed unanimously the stereotypical gender roles of boys and girls in the family unit, the perception of the household as inclusive of an extended family, and the pervasive attitude of maintaining secrecy about abusive practices and sexual assaults.

Participants from MINUSTAH as well as representatives of the Ministry of Justice contributing to this research contended that in Haiti, as in other countries affected by postconflict or sociopolitical crises, violence often arises from a shift of the gender system under heavy economic, social, and political pressures. When men's ability to find work in legitimate income-generating activities is lost, the economic decline of Haitian society ends up undermining men's role and identity. In these shifts of gender roles, power is expressed in multiple ways: through machismo and aspirational male sublimation as well as, in its most extreme form, through structural violence in the household and community (Maternowska 2006, 70). While indigence and unemployment significantly diminish male sources of self-esteem, sexual violence becomes a tool for reclaiming men's identity and overcoming their emasculation. "Rape . . . is a way of 'preserving tradition'" (Altman 2001), and in the case of Haitian men, who are fast losing all of their traditional roles in society, this makes unfortunate sense. It is clear, too, that through acts of violence and rape, men are responding to the structural systems—both political and economic—that control them. Violence in its many forms is a way of reasserting the eroding male identity" (Maternowska 2006, 70).

Victims' stories revealed that the impact of gender roles on their decision making was threefold. First, the internalization of gender stereotypes determined a victims' attitude to accept the assault as an inevitable byproduct of the socioeconomic collapse in Haitian communities and the troubled state of men. Second, women victims of sexual violence failed to take any action because they were conscious that holding relatives, intimates, or even gang members accountable would have been socially unacceptable. Third, women's fear of being stigmatized and abandoned by husbands or partners and of being subject to reprisals against either their families or themselves paralyzed any genuine attempt to ask for help and justice.

The following story of a twenty-seven-year-old rape victim interviewed in this study exemplifies girls' and women's fear of social stigmatization and rejection by their own families and community:

> Tamara is a merchant. She also manages to look after her husband and their two children of six and eight years of age, respectively. Every day she goes to the poor area of Martissant to sell her merchandise at the local market. One day, she went to the market and earned 125.000 *gourdes* from a client. On her way back home, two young men around twenty years old approached her, dragging her into a car parked at the corner of the street where two other men were waiting. The four men were members of one of the armed groups of the area responsible for many kidnappings. Tamara was kidnapped by the group for twenty-two days, beaten and gang raped multiple times per day. Upon the payment of 150.000 *gourdes,* she was finally released and abandoned at the edge of the street. Initially, she was so weak that she could not even walk and, thus, remained there for a while listening to cruel comments made about her by the passers-by. Fearing to be abandoned by her husband and rejected by her community, Tamara decided to keep quiet about the aggression. She refused to go to the hospital or to consult a doctor. Her injuries still hurt.

Another rape victim, who instead decided to ask for medical assistance at the GHESKIO medical center in Port-au-Prince and discovered that she had contracted HIV, reported having been rejected by her family. Her father held her responsible for the rape, and her aunt threw her out of the home. After the assault, she attempted to kill herself several times until she was finally committed to a psychiatric institution (Panos-Caraibes 2007, 16).

According to representatives of ENFOFANM, one of the most activist women's associations in the country, "Gender stereotypes, which have striking psychological and cultural connotations, are at the base of violence against women. Power relationships become entrenched in a definitive hierarchical order. On the basis of social differences between men and women in roles, behavior, and mental and emotional structures, women find themselves at the bottom of the hierarchy" (Merlet 2002, 168). The socialization of boys and girls through stereotypical notions, the expectations to comply with the asymmetrical models of gender roles, and the isolation and silence imposed on the victims of sexual abuse and violence significantly impinge on the reporting of rape cases. Such gender stereotypes ultimately strengthen the social understanding that violence against girls and women is a normal, everyday fact that needs to be accepted with a low threshold of tolerance and conceived of as a natural expression of Haitian culture.

Police Response

Victims' accounts of their engagement with police forces revealed a common pattern of further victimization against girls and women who report sexual assaults. Ridiculed and blamed by the officers receiving them at the police station immediately after the assault, they are often discouraged from lodging complaints or even dismissed in the first place either because rape is perceived as a nonserious crime or because, especially if the violence occurred within the family domain or was committed by acquaintances of the victim, rape is regarded as an unfortunate event that needs to be settled among the parties involved as a strictly private matter. This critical assessment of victims' interaction with the enforcement system confirms once more the pattern of discriminatory norms and gendered stereotypes plaguing Haitian society.

However, rape victims who did not report the assault to the police displayed an overwhelming distrust of the system and the conviction that the authorities would have not believed them or have protected them from retaliation, but, on the contrary, that they themselves would have been blamed for the attack and would not be able to contend with the court process. As a rape victim interviewed by Human Rights Watch put it, going to the police and pressing charges would be the equivalent of a "death wish" (Human Right Watch and the Coalition for Haitian Refugees 1994, 18).

Informants from the MINUSTAH Child Protection Unit and the ICRC contended also that victims fear not only being humiliated and derided by police officers but possibly being subject to further acts of violence from the security forces themselves. Behind the police station's closed doors, where depravation and brutality take place to the extent that fifteen-year-old girls entering the prison as virgins become pregnant by police officers while they are in custody, victims themselves often feel less secure than in the middle of the street.

Accounts from civil society organizations that rescue rape victims in Port-au-Prince reported that, in many cases, policemen themselves are responsible for the assaults, using their weapons to intimidate and threaten the victims. For instance, SOFA gave accounts of the tragic experience of one of their patients (SOFA 2007, 15):

> The young woman was a victim of the aggression during the night of November 19, 2006, in the area of Carrefour, in the southern part of the capital. That night the victim was at a friend's party. When she left, a policeman and his accomplices followed her down the street and attacked her, smashing her against the wall and beating her with a firearm. . . . The aggressors raped and sodomized the woman for several hours. In the end, although she tried to wriggle herself out of their control, the men lifted up her legs and lacerated her flesh from the vagina to the anus with a razor.

Similarly, Kay Fanm reported the case of one its patients who was brutally attacked by a policeman as she was entering her domicile (2007, 40). The man threatened the victim with his weapon, dragged her to the bedroom, tied her to the bed, and raped her. Soon after, the policeman called his six accomplices, who also raped the woman one after the other. After the multiple attacks, the policeman threatened the victim with death if she decided to report the assault.

A professor of sociology at the University of Port-au-Prince who agreed to participate in this study explained that women living in the slums profoundly distrust the security forces. In fact, they reckon that either police officers are not willing to enter the conflict zones to eradicate armed violence, or if they do enter those areas, they become the first ones responsible for wrongdoings and assaults against women and girls. Victims of sexual violence involved with the armed groups who participated in this study confirmed that not only do they prefer not to seek police protection but they even intentionally avoid security forces.

Some women who were in custody at the female prison of Port-au-Prince charged with association with malefactors claimed during their interviews that they had been randomly arrested during police raids in the slums, even though they were not involved in armed violence. Some of them lamented that they just happened to be in the area targeted for the security operation.

A representative of UNPOL reported that a project has been designed but not yet funded to train female police officers of the PNH on gender issues and to make them responsible for receiving rape victims' complaints and for dealing with women associated with armed groups in detention. However, few female police officers have been hired so far. Moreover, few police stations have provided their female employees with training courses on gender issues, most of which have been discontinued because of monetary shortages.

Specifically for girls, the two sections of the Brigade de Protection des Mineurs within the PNH—the section responsible for minors who are victims of abuse and maltreatment and the section for domestic violence—are designed to search for, investigate, identify, and arrest instigators and perpetrators as well as accomplices and facilitators of, *inter alia*, sexual violence and abuse against girls and restavèks (Sananes 2007). Established in 2002 and inaugurated on May 23, 2003, as a specialized unit of the Central Directorate of the Judiciary Police, the Brigade de Protection des Mineurs is not simply a functional division within the security system but, rather, a specific institution financed by UNICEF and the French Development Agency and aimed at the implementation of the international requirements under the Convention on the Rights of the Child for the prevention and repression of violence committed by minors or against them.

According to an evaluation of the unit, out of the 250 infractions reported and delivered from May 2003 to November 2006, 105 of them (46 percent) were rape cases (Sananes 2007). Despite efforts to respond effectively to increasing juvenile delinquency and the widespread and systematic sexual violence against girls in Port-au-Prince, the Brigade de Protection des Mineurs is challenged by the lack of capacity, resources, and specialized personnel as well as the decadence and corruption in the national security system.

Criminal-Justice Response

The Haitian judicial system has been affected by corruption, dysfunction, and forced military intrusions throughout the history of the Republic. Any attempt, no matter how feeble, to improve the standards of the criminal-justice institutions and proceedings has been subverted, first, by the two Duvalier dictatorships; subsequently, by the bloody military coup; and, finally, by decline and degradation during the last Aristide government.

In the current climate, due process and judicial redress in criminal proceedings are extremely difficult to obtain. Few cases are adjudicated each year, and prisoners are commonly held for lengthy periods without trial or sentencing. The resolution of these cases often depends more on money and power than on justice. Poverty, corruption, and abusive decisions interfere at every stage of the judicial process, from the investigation of a case to the decision; such interference intimidates the people involved and compromises the independence, transparency, and performance of judges, prosecutors, and attorneys.

In this situation, rape is not an exception to the prevalent rule of impunity for human-rights violations in Haiti. A memoir from a UN Civilian Mission's former director of legal services in 1994 is still an accurate portrayal of the current situation:

> A system that already is so rife with intimidation, bribery, corruption, and outside pressures cannot ensure that victims' rights will be respected, and that perpetrators of assaults will be punished in accordance with the law. Even in business disputes and other simple crimes, there is just too much room for something to go wrong. There is no reason for anyone, and especially a victim of rape . . . to believe that there is a chance for judicial redress. It won't just happen. Furthermore, the woman would probably be putting her life in danger. It is no accident that the justice system in Haiti does not work. The government has fostered this and benefits from it. (Human Rights Watch and the National Coalition for Haitian Refugees 1994, 17)

Judges and prosecutors interviewed for this study claimed that the inefficiency and unresponsiveness of the system originate in the lack of capacity and resources, the low salaries that compel them to have more than one job, and the external and intimidating pressures that put their own lives at stake. Justices from the Tribunal des Mineurs (Tribunal for Minors), established on 1961 near Bel Air, who are responsible for offenses and crimes committed by minors from the age of thirteen to sixteen, deplored the fact that the violence that overwhelms the capital has prevented the regular functioning of the court and the everyday access to their workplace for judges and administrative personnel.

Advocates from Human Rights Watch reported the view of the president of the Port-au-Prince Bar Association: "If a [raped] woman belongs to a wealthy family, the family will finance the investigation. They can put a car and money at the disposal of the police. The policemen will have an incentive to conduct a thorough investigation. However, if the woman is from the lower class and does not know the [identity of the rapist], the police will have no car, no gas. . . . It is all so expensive. It will be a difficult situation for the girl" (Human Rights Watch and the National Coalition for Haitian Refugees 1994, 18). Police officers from the PNH and the Brigade de Protection des Mineurs who took part in this study confirmed that the lack of basic resources and services, including cars, computers, telephones, and electricity, severely impede investigations and arrests. Financial means also have an important impact on the legal assistance for victims. In Haiti, only wealthy families can afford to hire good attorneys, whereas girls from low-income households and deprived communities are left to depend on state legal-aid trainees, who have just graduated from law school and who intervene at the trial without enough experience and influence to defend their clients' interests effectively.

Given limited funds and no information about the competencies and functions of judicial institutions, the very poor, who need the law the most, commonly resort to informal mechanisms of dispute resolution. "Disputes are normally resolved in either of two ways: by brute force or bribery. In any event, it is not the custom of the people, and especially women, to use lawyers and the judicial system. The law has never protected women. The solution is to bribe someone who is in power and, in cases of political rape, you would be bargaining with the devil" (Human Rights Watch and the National Coalition for Haitian Refugees 1994, 18). Interviews conducted with judges of the Tribunal des Mineurs revealed that informal instruments of justice include private retaliation by means of brutal force, reconciliation through the "wise discernment" of the chief of the community, as well as fetishism and voodoo ceremonies to evoke natural spirits and demand revenge. Representatives of KOFAVIV reported that the only form of community justice in the slums is barbaric retaliation against the assailants. They recalled the case of a ten-year-old girl who was brutally raped by a bandit in the slum of Martissant. The population was outraged by the feral aggression. Members of a vigilante group operating in the area reacted by splitting the head of the rapist open.

Justices and representatives of the Ombudsman Haiti contend that rape is a crime to be settled man-to-man outside the courtroom, even by the parents themselves, who are often willing to dismiss the cases out of desperation as soon as they receive a small reimbursement; victims, however, lament that "money often pays other hands to shuck off the case." A victim interviewed in this study reported having been raped twice by members of different armed groups. The first time, she decided to report the attack to authorities through the legal assistance provided by Kay Fanm. The case was taken before the Tribunal of Port-au-Prince, but it was soon dismissed; the assailants were released after the payment of a bribe by the assailants' families to the judge in charge of the case. The second time she was raped, the victim understandably decided there was no point in reporting the assault.

When seeking justice for the assaults committed against them, girls and women in Haiti confront not only a corrupt and inefficient judicial system but also procedural hurdles to gathering the evidence necessary to support a rape allegation. Required to provide a medical certificate verifying that forcible sexual intercourse has occurred, the majority of victims, terrified of reprisals against their families or themselves, struggle to reach hospitals or other institutions that are often located a long way from their shantytowns.

> In Haiti, without a certificate confirming rape, a woman may try to proceed with filing a charge, but it will be exceedingly difficult, bordering on the impossible. It is not that she cannot file a complaint. It is that the complaint will go nowhere, or in the countryside, where medical certificates are difficult to get due to the absence of doctors, the judge hearing the case will be able to wield incredible discretionary power regarding the type of questions he subjects the women to. Without the corroborating evidence, it is the woman's word against the man's and she is bound to lose. (Human Rights Watch and the National Coalition for Haitian Refugees 1994, 20)

Participants from the Ministry for the Status of Women emphasized that girls from remote areas of the country or the deprived slums of the capital often arrive at the hospital too late to demonstrate that forcible sexual intercourse has occurred, or, even worse, they are provided with medical certificates that eventually prove to be incomplete or illegible. Although a protocol of agreement providing free medical certificates to rape victims was signed by the Ministry for the Status of Women, the Ministry of Justice, and the Ministry of Public Health on November 17, 2006 (St. Fleur 2006; SOFA 2007, 87), the practical obstacles and perils women face in trying to reach hospitals or private doctors are still far from being overcome.

Aggregate data from URAMEL and MDM show that between 2002 and 2005, out of 372 victims of sexual violence, 76.1 percent were minors and only 23.9 percent were adult women (see Table de Concertation Nationale sur les Violences Faites aux Femmes 2005a). Yet, data from SOFA collected between 2003 and 2005 revealed that all the victims who visited the police and pressed charges after the attack were minors. Participants in this study from the MINUSTAH Gender Unit explained that in Haiti it is easier to report a case of sexual violence against a girl than against a woman because a woman is more exposed to shame and social reprobation. While young girls are perceived to be innocent victims, adult women are often blamed or held accountable for the assault.

Another pertinent explanation for the significant disparity between girls and adult women in the reporting of sexual violence is based on the social understanding that rape is a crime only when it is committed against a virgin. The patriarchal misconceptions and gender bias that lead to classifying a girl's body as the property of the family and as a commodity to be transferred from man to man still deeply pervade Haitian culture and society. Although judges interviewed for this study declared that no distinction is made before the law, victims revealed that in practice anyone who alleges rape must endure public scrutiny of her own virtue. International organizations and national women's associations denounce the fact that raping a nonvirgin, whose honor has been already compromised, is commonly considered a less serious offense. Rape charges by nonvirgin victims are often dismissed, as if, because of their previous sexual experiences, they could no longer be raped but would just consent to any further sexual contacts.

With respect to women and girls associated with armed groups, the Haitian judicial system holds them accountable for the general charge of association with malefactors as accomplices of the wrongdoers. Internal dysfunction within the justice system and the lack of legal aid relegate these women and girls to wait in custody, often for years, before obtaining a fair trial. Deprived of any legal assistance and basic legal rights, "they can only hope for a miracle," declared a representative of UNICEF Haiti working with children in conflict with the law.

A judge working at the Tribunal of Port-au-Prince reported that, fearing arrest, many women and girls who are victims of sexual violence by gangs but then decide to join the armed groups do not report the assaults to authorities regardless of whether they were forcibly recruited by the groups or were willing to cooperate with the justice system. Admittedly, the prospect of being in detention seems horrifying in Haiti because women and girls are often further victims of sexual violence either by police officers or by other female inmates while in custody. In fact, social service workers as well as the director of the female prison in Port-au-Prince who agreed to participate in this study reported that young inmates are sometimes victims of sexual violence perpetrated by their older peers, who reproduce the hierarchical structures and brutal retaliation of the armed groups inside the prison.

Judicial Developments after 2005

Data collected from Kay Fanm provide information about the following proceedings, which succeeded in providing judicial redress to the claimants. Representatives of Kay Fanm interviewed for this study declared that two principal motivations encouraged the women involved to report the assault: first, victims were supported by their families when they embarked on the painful process of making reports to the authorities; and, second, victims could benefit from legal aid that was provided by the organization and was funded through international programs. None of the cases below focused on victims who were somehow involved in armed violence. So far, in Haiti, no organizations provide legal aid to women and girls in detention who have been accused of association with malefactors.

The first case involves an attack committed by a police officer, James Montas, against a twenty-year-old woman, Carline Séide, as she was entering her house in Delmas 19, Port-au-Prince, on November 2, 2003 (Kay Fanm 2007, 40). Montas threatened and beat the victim with his weapon, dragged her to the bedroom, and, after having handcuffed her to the bed, raped her. Subsequently, Montas called his six accomplices, who also raped the woman one after the other. Following the multiple attacks, the policeman threatened the victim with death if she reported the attack.

In spite of the intimidation, Séide resolved to report the assault to authorities and to pursue legal action with the assistance of Kay Fanm. On August 3, 2006, the case was adjudicated by the Criminal Court of Port-au-Prince. The public prosecutor requested the penalty of unlimited detention for the police officer in compliance with Articles 279 and 281 of the Haitian Penal Code. In fact, according to Article 281, if the rape is committed by an individual who has abused his or her authority, the maximum penalty should be applied. However, the defense requested the immediate and unconditional release of Montas, arguing that he was victim of a conspiracy.

The final verdict, released by Judge Jean Carvez on August 8, 2006, condemned the accused to six years of detention. The sentence acknowledged that the weapon and handcuffs used by the police officer during the assault were found in his residence; the crime was perpetrated with free deliberation, violence, and lack of the victim's consent; and the medical certificate, issued by the Hospital of the State University of Haiti (General Hospital), confirmed the injuries and the penetration of the victim. Although the public prosecutor requested the maximum penalty for the accused in compliance with the Haitian Penal Code, the judge decided to condemn him to six years of imprisonment. Representatives of Kay Fanm who participated in this study reported that despite the reduction of the penalty, this rape case was the only one successfully prosecuted in 2006 and, thus, held symbolic importance for the struggle to eradicate violence against women in Haiti.

The Kay Fanm representatives also reported that, similarly in 2007, a second rape case was successfully prosecuted with a substantial reduction in the penalty. The case involved a twelve-year-old girl who was brutally raped by a neighbor. The man, who was an electrician and knew the girl and her mother very well, entered the victim's home while she was taking a shower. He drugged her and brutally raped her until she fainted. When the girl regained consciousness she found blood between her legs. The public prosecutor requested the permanent detention of the assailant considering the fact that the victim was a minor. However, the judge sentenced the man to only fifteen years in prison.

In 2008, two more rape cases were adjudicated in Port-au-Prince with the legal assistance of Kay Fanm. The first one involved a twenty-seven-year-old woman who was attacked by an armed group as she was leaving a Protestant church in 2005. The group dragged the victim to a nearby cemetery, forced her to walk naked around the graves, and viciously raped her. Only one of the assailants was successfully prosecuted and sentenced to nine years of detention.

The other case regarded a fifteen-year-old girl who was attacked by a fifty-one-year-old man in the city of Leogane. The victim was going to visit her father when she was kidnapped by her assailant in the middle of the street. The man kept the girl for an entire week, raping her multiple times per day. The judge asserted that since the victim did not scream at the moment of the attack, she had consented to the sexual relationship. Therefore, the man was not held accountable of either for the kidnapping or for the rape but only for having engaged in a consensual sexual relationship with a minor, which was punishable by two years of imprisonment. The director of Kay Fanm, who reported the case during the interview, on the one hand, lamented the gender bias that still pervades the criminal-justice system in Haiti but, on the other hand, acknowledged that any condemnation of rape, even with the lowest penalty, was an important achievement in the struggle of Haitian activists to eradicate gender-based violence.

This chapter describes rape victims' challenges and subsequent decision-making processes in seeking help. Their reluctance to report assaults to authorities indicates the severe impact gender bias has on the security and judicial systems in Haiti, the inadequacies of these systems, the widespread lack of law enforcement, and the resulting impact on women's decisions not to report rape. Given such shortcomings, the following chapter suggests practical strategies for change in order to effectively protect Haitian women and girls from gender-based violence and from being recruited by the armed groups as they attempt to find self-defense and coping mechanisms for themselves and their families.

6

Strategies for Action

Despite the pervasive structures of gender inequality in Haitian society, some women actively resist subordination and violence. By presenting an account of their efforts to counter gender-based violations and to reclaim equality and protection for their daughters and themselves, the following analysis identifies promising approaches and programs employed by the nonprofit organizations and civil society associations devoted to advancing human rights for women in the country. This chapter suggests that only by implementing long-term, cooperative, and multilateral approaches with local resources and decision making can international organizations operating in the country successfully convey human-rights principles in a practical context and, in so doing, serve their ultimate purpose.

Women's Struggle in Haiti

Since the fall of the two Duvalier dictatorships, women's organizations have sprung up on the Haitian political scene as the renaissance of the Mouvement des Femmes Haitiennes (Haitian Women's Movement). On April 3, 1986, three hundred thousand women poured into the streets of Port-au-Prince and several provincial towns demanding their participation in the government's decision making as well as a political agenda concerning women's poverty and sexual violence (Magloire 2004, 68). A few years later, during the military regime of 1991–1994, the issue of violence became one of the primary spearheads in mobilizing Haitian women's associations against the widespread and systematic use of rape as a political weapon. At that time, a coalition of more than one hundred women's organizations convened the First National Meeting Opposing Violence against Women, in which more than three hundred victims shared their painful memories and established a resistance movement (Merlet 2002, 169).

The struggle against violence affecting women finally emerged on the national political agenda in 1997, when, because of the disinterest of the government in providing victims with adequate justice, women's associations held the International Tribunal on Violence against Haitian Women (see United Nations Economic and Social Council 2000). During the three-day sessions of the tribunal, an international panel of judges heard testimony from rape victims; proposed recommendations for addressing political violence, domestic violence, and sexual violence against women in the country; and declared the shortcomings of the judicial and security systems as well as of the social and public-health services to be of great concern.

Representatives of several women's organizations—some of whom are victims themselves—interviewed for this study confirmed having joined their associations at the time of the military coup. Believing in the reconciliatory and relieving power of their narratives before the tribunal, they hoped to obtain judicial redress and compensation. Nevertheless, despite the return to constitutional order in Haiti in 1994, victims of political violence never obtained any redress, justice, or financial support from the government. Nowadays they have simply exhausted their hopes but continue to commit their efforts to opposing the very foundations of women's oppression as well as in building equal and democratic institutions. However, the collapse of the expectations for the tribunal left those women's associations operating on a community scale with the profound conviction that claiming justice for sexual violence is a vain effort and convinced them to organize instead to provide victims with primary medical assistance.

The most recent experiment is that of the Table de Concertation Nationale sur les Violences Faites aux Femmes, established in December 2003 on the initiative of the UNFPA in consultation with other agencies of the UN system and of international cooperation, the Ministry for the Status of Women, the Ministry of Public Heath, the Ministry of Justice, and several civil society organizations. In November 2005, the Table de Concertation Nationale finalized a national plan for the period 2006–2011 aimed at addressing all forms of violence against women and establishing a unique forum of international and national partners to develop concrete strategic actions (Table de Concertation Nationale sur les Violences Faites aux Femmes 2005a). Informants from the MINUSTAH Gender Unit, as part of the Table de Concertation Nationale, highlighted the potential of the committee to combine different perspectives and approaches but also emphasized the challenge of reaching an agreement among so many different partners on effective responses to violence against women.

Women Living without Violence

The following discussion surveys policy and legal recommendations at both the international and national level to address gender-based violence. Moreover, interventions at the community level are suggested to ensure women's participation in the Haitian public domain as well as in the reconciliation and peace-making processes.

International Commitments

Although the government of Haiti has ratified most of the important conventions mentioned in Chapter 4, there is still a long road ahead. To begin, as recommended by the Special Rapporteur on violence against women in 2000 (United Nations Economic and Social Council 2000), the government of Haiti should ratify without delay the Convention against Torture and Other Cruel, Inhuman, or Degrading Treatment or Punishment as well as the Inter-American Convention to Prevent and Punish Torture.[1] Specifically for children, the Haitian government should commit to promptly ratifying the Optional Protocols to the Convention on the Rights of the Child on the involvement of children in armed conflict and on the sale of children, child prostitution, and child pornography.[2]

In addition to ratifying such international conventions, Haiti should immediately comply with its existing obligations under human-rights law by harmonizing all relevant domestic-law provisions with international standards and by reporting the results to the treaty-monitoring bodies. The recommendation of the Special Rapporteur on violence against women to the government of Haiti to cooperate with nongovernmental and women's organizations in preparing a consolidated comprehensive report to the Committee on the Elimination of Discrimination against Women was instituted only in 2009 after a long delay. Representatives of the MINUSTAH Gender Unit interviewed for this study reaffirmed the fact that the preparation of the report was one of the primary goals of their agenda. Along the same lines, representatives of the MINUSTAH Child Protection Unit affirmed their intent to cooperate with NGOs and civil society associations in preparing the first report to the Committee on the Rights of the Child as well as to promote the ratification by the Haitian government of both of the Optional Protocols to the Convention itself.

It is indeed critical that the Republic of Haiti ratify the Rome Statute as well as the Optional Protocols in order to make state and nonstate actors accountable for the recruitment and use of children in hostilities, regardless of their direct or indirect involvement in armed violence. As mentioned, the UN Special Representative of the Secretary-General for Children and Armed Conflict has declared that "there is no universally applicable definition of armed conflict" (United Nations General Assembly/ Security Council 2006) and instead has espoused a pragmatic and cooperative approach to this issue, focusing on ensuring broad and effective protection for children exposed to situations of concern, regardless of the definition of the term *armed conflict.*

Based on the grave violations committed against children in Haiti, including sexual violence against girls and their recruitment into armed groups, the Special Representative has included Haiti among the countries listed in the 2006 and 2007 reports to the Secretary-General on children and armed conflict (United Nations General Assembly 2006; United Nations General Assembly 2007). According to the empirical evidence presented in this study, the pragmatic and extensive interpretation of the term *armed conflict* has become ever more pertinent in the Haitian context. Indeed, the findings have revealed not only that gender-based violence is widespread and systematically perpetrated but also that female aggression is principally employed as a coping response to previous victimization and as an adaptive strategy to the daily hardships women and girls face in the context of armed violence.

Therefore, if female participation in the gangs is understood as a survival strategy, current Haitian legislation that provides solely for girls' and women's prosecution for the offense of association with malefactors is at the very least inadequate. The point is not that those who engage in violence should be unaccountable but rather that DDR programs should be designed for the social rehabilitation and reintegration of female victims.

Disarmament, Demobilization, and Reintegration Programs

The legal basis for the establishment and development of DDR programs has been laid out in several international legal instruments. Specifically, Resolution 1325 on Women, Peace, and Security, adopted by the UN Security Council in 2000, has called on all actors involved in peace-settlement negotiations to adopt a gender perspective and to take into account girls' and women's needs during rehabilitation, reintegration, and postconflict reconstruction.[3]

In particular, measures to be adopted should support local women's peace initiatives and indigenous peace processes for conflict resolution as well as involve women in all implementation mechanisms of the peace agreements. Moreover, such measures should ensure the protection and respect for human rights of women and girls, particularly as they relate to the constitution, the electoral system, the police, and the judiciary. Furthermore, reasserting the fact that women can be not only victims of but also actors in war, Resolution 1325 encourages all those involved in planning for DDR to consider the unique needs of female and male ex-combatants.

Similarly, the Convention on the Rights of the Child provides that member states shall take all appropriate measures to promote the physical and psychological recovery as well as the social reintegration of child victims of armed conflict and other forms of abuse (art. 39).[4] Along the same line, over seventy-eight member states, including Haiti, have expressed their full commitment to the Paris Principles, which provide guidelines regarding DDR of all categories of children associated with armed groups (United Nations International Children's Emergency Fund 2007).

The Paris Principles have clarified that coercing girls into marriage, forced sexual relations, domestic labor, or logistical support in armed conflict constitutes recruitment and, thus, is contrary to fundamental human rights and humanitarian law. This clarification has finally solved the critical question of whether girls who are indirectly involved in a conflict because their roles are not related to weapons can still benefit from specific programs aimed at their rehabilitation and reintegration into society. Furthermore, the Paris Principles assert that DDR programs for girls should ensure that their specific needs are met, including safe and private accommodations with separate facilities, measures for their safety and protection in residential settings, support for girl mothers, and education and opportunities to develop skills and generate income in nonexploitative settings.

In detail, women and girls associated with armed groups are eligible for registration and participation in DDR program based on the following criteria (United Nations Department of Peacekeeping Operations 2004):

- Women and girls who have engaged directly in fighting either as combatants or as health personnel (Helland et al. 1999).
- Women and girls who have either voluntarily or coercively provided support functions in an armed group. Such functions can include carrying supplies and weapons, working as cooks and cleaners, serving as concubines or sexual slaves.
- Women and girls who are spouses or are otherwise dependents of both male and female ex-combatants. For the purposes of the DDR programs, a dependent is anyone living in an ex-combatant's household and under his/her care. This may include spouses, partners, children, parents, siblings, and members of the extended family.

As emphasized by Resolution 1325 as well as the Paris Principles, women and girls who are either ex-combatants or who have provided support functions for armed groups have specific needs. These can relate to health issues, child care, or social stigmatization by their families and communities during the reintegration process. Moreover, women and girls who have been abducted, sexually assaulted or raped, or forced into marriage, prostitution, or sexual slavery may need psychological assistance as well as further protection, including protection from re-recruitment.

Although the adoption of both Resolution 1325 and the Paris Principles is a significant political initiative and represents a shared commitment by the international community, unfortunately these two legal instruments are not legally binding on member states; thus, it has been difficult to enforce them effectively. In practice, one of the main obstacles to females' inclusion in the DDR programs is the fact that because they are usually not provided with weapons, they cannot return arms in exchange for reintegration assistance. Other reasons may include having less access to news sources, having lower literacy skills than their male peers, and bearing the stigma of having been victims of sexual violence or affiliates of armed groups. Worldwide statistics have confirmed the fact that only approximately 2 percent of girls are included in DDR programs, whereas at least 40 percent of them participate or have participated in conflicts and armed violence (Hobson 2005).

Several authors have suggested that in order to extend eligibility as beneficiaries of the programs to women and girls who are indirectly involved in armed violence, the reintegration component should be detached from disarmament and demobilization (Pillai 2008). Others have emphasized the need to strengthen the psychological and social factors inherent in reintegration and rehabilitation, rather than focusing exclusively on the economic and educational aspects. Further weaknesses in the DDR programs have been reported by informants of this study who have declared that one of the remaining challenges is how to create living options and concrete opportunities for women and girls on their return to their own communities.

National Strategy for Disarmament, Violence Reduction, and Community Security

Despite the adoption of the National Strategy for Disarmament, Violence Reduction, and Community Security by the Haitian government in 2006, little has been done in this regard since that time. The National Strategy's vision included the express intent of prioritizing the special needs of women and children associated with armed groups, including reintegration support for women who also have been victims of gender-based violence and the promotion of their key role in achieving peaceful forms of conflict mediation.[5]

In particular, the National Strategy was designed to foster consultation and cooperation with relevant international partners, including UNICEF, to ensure that the best interests of the child are consistently respected in all areas of programming. Moreover, in order to reduce the financial vulnerability of women associated with armed groups to transactional sex and rape as well as to enhance their ability to contribute to community conflict management, the National Strategy targeted a portion of microgrant and training opportunities specifically for them. However, DDR programs for these women have rarely been implemented, are usually underfunded, and, thus, have rapidly disappeared. Equally unsuccessful and apparently a low priority has been female inclusion in DDR programs designed for male combatants.

Such programs for women and girls involved in armed violence in Haiti should include the following practices during the three phases of disarmament, demobilization, and reintegration. In particular, during the disarmament process, women and girls associated with armed groups are often excluded from the lists of combatants to be demobilized, perhaps because women and girls themselves choose not to come forward because of the stigma of having been raped by the gangs and then being associated with the groups during peacetime. In other cases, they may not receive information about their eligibility to participate in the DDR programs, or their male peers may intentionally exclude them from the lists, believing that their share of demobilization benefits may be reduced if additional individuals register.

Therefore, efforts should be made to determine the exact number of women and girls involved in armed violence in Haiti as well as the roles they have played in the groups. Possible ways of accomplishing this include hiring female interpreters and researchers to interview women and girls associated with the gangs as well as ensuring that media and public-information campaigns reach out to female beneficiaries by providing a clear indication of their eligibility to participate in the DDR programs. Program planners should organize separate accommodations and sanitary facilities for women and girls. Once they are registered, the information they provide should be disaggregated by sex and age to ensure that the specific needs of women and girls will be respected in the demobilization and reintegration phases of the DDR programs.

During the demobilization phase, special attention should be paid to the following issues. Benefits packages provided to beneficiaries of the programs should include both financial and material resources as well as basic professional training. In particular, the general aim must be to ensure an equal distribution of benefits packages to enable women and girls to have the same economic options as their male peers as they are reintegrated into society. These packages could include microfinance support for businesses as well as resource allocation for literacy and training in high-earning skills for women and girls. Health care, rehabilitation facilities, and counseling services should be provided to female beneficiaries who have been abducted, raped, or sexually enslaved by armed groups. Child-care facilities should also be available for mothers participating in the programs.

Finally, during the reintegration phase the National Strategy and its partners should consider the following gender perspectives related to the economic and social reinsertion of women and girls into Haitian society. The fact that women may have fewer job opportunities than their male peers has serious implications if they are the main providers for their dependents. Therefore, program planners should ensure that female beneficiaries have equal training and employment opportunities by allocating funding for child care and organizing vocational training as close as possible to the areas where women and girls reside. These measures will minimize irregular attendance because of family constraints and transportation and mobility problems. Economic reintegration should also include a monitoring mechanism to track women and girls during their reinsertion into society as well as to identify their challenges and to periodically readjust the DDR programs accordingly.

Especially for women and girls who have been victims of sexual violence by the gangs social reintegration may be difficult. They are likely to face rejection or denigration by their own families and communities. Therefore, public awareness, sensitization campaigns, and reconciliation messages should be designed to alleviate the plight of women and girls who may have suffered abuse while with armed groups as well as to help them readjust to a peaceful life. The National Strategy and its partners should also encourage the establishment of civil society organizations specifically devoted to the disarmament and rehabilitation of women and girls associated with armed groups in Haiti. Their intervention at the community level in reaching out to rape victims affiliated with the groups as well as in sensitizing their families and neighbors will also be crucial for effectively implementing DDR programs in the country.

National Interventions

Despite the need for the Haitian government to ratify and comply with internationals treaties and commitments as a first step toward the fulfillment of those standards, effective advancement of human rights for girls and women in the country cannot be accomplished without a multipronged approach among the different institutional actors, functions, and sectors of the nation-state. Therefore, proper implementation of international-law dictates and benchmarks cannot deviate too far from specific strategies and measures of intervention at the various levels of society.

Legislative Measures

Although the adoption of the Decret Modifiant le Régime des Agressions Sexuelles et Éliminant en la Matière les Discriminations contre la Femme (Decree Changing the Regulation of Sexual Aggression and Eliminating Forms of Discrimination against Women) in July 2005 represented a significant step toward compliance with international human-rights standards, the Haitian government still must introduce comprehensive legislation on domestic violence condemning, among other practices, the sexual abuse and exploitation of girls. Informants from Ombudsman Haiti contended that the resistance to adopting such legislation is based on the low threshold of tolerance for violence and abuse perpetrated inside the household, the customary belief that the law should never interfere in family matters, and the social understanding that severe discipline and violent correction need to be applied to girls and women for their own good.

The implementation of an official mechanism for the collection and analysis of national data on violence against girls and women is a mandatory reform for an accurate assessment of the real nature and extent of the problem facing Haitian society. Representatives of the Ministry for the Status of Women participating in this study emphasized that the extant lack of official national statistics significantly compromises any attempt to raise awareness and to promote the political legitimacy of the issue. A successful campaign for the adoption of comprehensive legislation on domestic violence as well as for the controversial decriminalization of abortion in rape cases cannot be pursued without reliable data on the high incidence of sexual violence and abuse against girls and women through-out the entire country.

With respect to women and girls involved in armed violence, the current Haitian legislation, which provides solely for their prosecution for the offense of association with malefactors, is inadequate. Consider-ing that most of these women and girls have been previously victimized by the gangs and still made the decision to join the groups and retaliate within the coercive context of armed violence, they should be eligible to participate in the DDR programs based on the international commitments undertaken by the Haitian government. To be sure, this is not to suggest that legal action should not be pursued against women and girls if they have indeed engaged in violence and are charged with other offenses, like kidnapping, extortion, or trafficking. Rather the point is to ensure that a fair investigation is conducted by the authorities to assess women's roles and effective involvement within the armed groups.

Law Enforcement

Because police forces are the primary institutional resort for rape victims, who may also be involved in armed violence, and the essential connection between the first report of a crime and the judicial system's responses, a concrete action plan should be implemented to improve the shortcomings and dysfunction that affect the security system. Indeed, several scholars argue that one of the main reasons for the surge of armed groups in Haiti is the lack of police intervention in the urban areas most affected by poverty and insecurity (Puechguirbal, Man, and Loutis 2009).

Findings presented in this study have revealed that many women resort to joining the vigilante groups to protect themselves and their fami-lies primarily in response to the public distrust of security forces and their lack of intervention in the slums. Indiscriminate police raids against the local population, the involvement of security officers in violence against women, as well as gender bias against victims contribute greatly to wom-en's reluctance to report an assault or to cooperate with the police regard-ing their association with the armed groups or both.

To start, given the crucial role that security forces could play in prevent-ing and addressing gender-based violence and women's violence within their own communities, representatives of the UNFPA who participated in this study asserted that the entire system for lodging complaints should be revised. Informants from several international and national institutions unanimously confirmed the urgency of providing police stations with a separate room in which rape victims, including those associated with armed groups, can be appropriately received and their complaints confidentially collected. Police officers should also undertake prompt and efficient follow-up to the reporting of a crime.

Together with the establishment of specific facilities for lodging complaints, extended police training (including components on women's human rights, violence against women, and women's violence) must be increased to strengthen the belief that police forces could and should act as agents for protection within their own communities. To that extent, close cooperation with the Ministry for the Status of Women and women's civil society associations engaged in the field may hasten the design of specialized and well-crafted training modules for police cadets as well as police officers already in service with respect to gender-based violence and appropriate responses.

The United Nations, through the specific involvement of the MINUSTAH Gender Unit, the MINUSTAH Child Protection Unit, and above all UNPOL, should play a crucial role in accompanying, monitoring, and guiding the Haitian national police in their work. They should also provide consistent and integrated police training on women's human rights as an essential contribution to increasing the reporting of sexual assaults and to designing strategies to combat gender-based violence and women's violence in the country.

The development of a plan for coordination of the Ministry for the Status of Women, the Ministry of Justice, and the PNH to elaborate a coherent multilateral approach to gender-based violence and women's violence remains fundamental. In particular, establishing a women's police unit comprised of female police officers responsible, among other duties, for receiving complaints and conducting investigations in cases of violence against women or women's involvement in armed violence is highly recommended.

On a larger scale, the recruitment of and participation of women in the police force is an important challenge for the Haitian security system. On December 18, 2006, out of 565 police cadets recruited only twenty-five

(4.4 percent) were women; and on February 5, 2007, despite the fact that out of 649 police cadets recruited, 78 were women and, therefore, the proportion increased to 12 percent compared with the previous year, the chief of police declared that women's presence in the national security system requires a "revolution in the Haitian mentality hard to be achieved" (Sananes 2007, 5). Representatives from the Brigade de Protection des Mineurs as well as from UNICEF interviewed for this study revealed that one of their objectives is increasing the female presence in the police forces to 25 percent. Because of the resistance to involving women in the process of capacity building within the security system, the adoption of an affirmative quota in their favor may be explored as well as the improvement of working conditions for female police officers, including their treatment by peers and commanders.

Informants from the Brigade de Protection des Mineurs and UNICEF pointed out the detrimental impact of a dysfunctional judiciary on the effectiveness of the security sector. It is necessary for police forces to develop a notion of working for an efficient system because ineffective, or lack of, follow-up by the judiciary of cases submitted by the police leads to demoralization, indifference, and an increase in human-rights violations. A multilateral and cooperative approach as well as more constructive and coherent relationships between police forces and the judiciary system are essential in order to provide adequate responses to gender-based violence and women's violence in Haiti.

As for the future of the police force, three structural challenges should be overcome in order to consolidate the role of the civilian police and to establish a respected tradition for the security system in Haiti: first, the politicization of the security force by political factions promoting their own purposes needs to be stopped; second, the widespread corruption, including that connected to drugs and other illicit activities, should be addressed; and third, significant efforts must be devoted to battling the active participation and involvement of members of the force in armed gangs. Therefore, effective responses should focus on discipline and the accountability of police forces.

Finally, according to a study conducted by UNICEF on the functioning of the Brigade de Protection des Mineurs, practical interventions and international aid should be employed to improve police officers' working conditions and to increase their limited financial resources. Recommendations for practical measures include the adoption of a radio and functioning telephone system; the installation of surveillance cameras in police stations and detention cells; the endowment of computers, cars, or motorcycles; the establishment of a specific fund to provide victims or minors who are arrested with food and primary assistance; and an effective and reliable system of referral for victims of rape and sexual abuse to competent international organizations and national institutions responsible for medical assistance and psychological support (Sananes 2007).

Criminal-Justice Reform

Considering the shortcomings and dysfunction of the Haitian criminal-justice system, representatives of the Ministry of Justice as well as magistrates from the Tribunal des Mineurs interviewed for this study recognized the pressing need for judiciary reforms in order to bring the inadequate national legislation and responses to gender-based violence and women's violence into harmony with Haiti's obligations under international human-rights instruments. Because the lack of an effective judicial system itself represents a major violation of human rights, a number of strategies for the future must be formulated. Efforts devoted to the general goal of modernizing the law and creating new legal instruments should be accompanied by improved judicial institutions devoid of corruption and decadence.

To that point, a concrete plan of action may begin, first, by devising a revised training curriculum for a new generation of judges, including the teaching of principles of women's human rights and of preventing domestic violence; second, by negotiating an increase in judges' salaries to attract newly qualified professionals in the judiciary sector and to preclude justices from undertaking other concurrent jobs or appointments to compensate for the limited income; and, third, by implementing an official and organized system of records and data collection for rape cases, perpetrators, victims, and women involved in armed violence. On a practical level, Haitian tribunals need to be endowed with resources and basic materials, such as computers and registries, in order to facilitate the justices' work and to encourage the improved performance of their duties.

Magistrates of Haitian ordinary tribunals as well as the Tribunal des Mineurs emphasized that it is mandatory to encourage communication and collaboration between the police force and the judiciary system. Inter-locutors revealed that to date the lack of communication between the two sectors has escalated to the point that mandates of arrest issued by judges are often disregarded and unattended to by the police; the only hint of collaboration between the two bodies is the initial dossier containing the allegation that the police send to the judiciary authority. Because of the lack of communications and negligence in compliance, magistrates com-plain that they need to identify perpetrators of violence by themselves, thus incurring personal danger. Being unable to proceed with the arrest, they often prefer to bring the parties together to reach a reasonable settle-ment of the case outside the courtroom.

Given the extensive recourse to informal dispute resolution, alterna-tive models for change, such as mediation and restorative justice, could be explored to, on the one hand, minister to victims' needs and concerns at both the individual and community level, including providing for their privacy, preservation of their relationships and networks, expenses, social security, and support; and, on the other hand, officially regulate informal mechanisms of dispute resolution, which often result in the corruption or intimidation of either the judges or the victims.

The social cohesion and strong sense of community existing in Haiti, as expressed in family and kinship networks and in social expectations and control, and the fear of stigmatization and reprisal are the primary reasons for victims' wanting to reach informal dispute settlements. To be sure, mediation in sexual-violence cases can amplify disparities among panel members. However, implementing mediation and restorative-justice mod-els in the criminal-justice system at the postadjudicative stage—after the offender has pled guilty—may be a first step toward accountability and restitution for crimes of sexual violence as well as a way to avoid the dys-functional and abusive practices that contribute to widespread impunity and denial of responsibility.

Other valid reasons for adopting such alternative models are to encourage and facilitate victims' participation in the process and to envis-age strategies of negotiation and solutions that do not victimize girls and women any further but rather empower the parties to take responsibility for the past and to set boundaries for future behavior. Finally, introduc-ing alternative models for dispute resolution within a larger framework of criminal-justice reforms may ultimately lead to a realistic and effective approach of intervention inherent in Haitian reality and to strengthening local support systems and resources.

Women's Participation in Politics

As previously noted, in studies conducted in other countries affected by armed conflict, violence contributes to the exclusion of women from the public domain, thus preventing their active participation in politics as well as in peace-building. In particular, the International Crisis Group, an NGO, highlighted the fact that insecurity and gender-based violence undermine the social fabric of a society and preclude women from taking an active role in postconflict reconstruction and, more generally, in the political life of their own country. In a report on women's peace-building in Sudan, Congo, and Uganda, the International Crisis Group asserted that "strategies to prevent violence against women during war are simultaneously strategies to protect women's participation in reconstruction and democracy-building in the aftermath" (International Crisis Group 2006, 17).

Similarly, Haitian scholars have reflected on women's subordination in the society, which translates into their depreciation and exclusion from the public sphere and decision-making processes regarding their personal security (Magloire 2004, 102). In the words of a representative of the Ministry for the Status of Women, who also participated in this research, "Violence against women, or even the threat of violence, maintains women in a state of fear or constant vulnerability and limits their movements, . . . their access to public spaces where they would feel safe, their social participation, their autonomy. Their access to full citizenship is denied." Furthermore, findings presented in this study have demonstrated that women who have been victimized and deprived of their basic entitlements often resort to retaliation and violence to carve out a safe and acceptable place in Haitian society for themselves.

In addition to public insecurity, the traditional sexual division of labor in Haiti prevents women from engaging in public life. Gender hierarchies define specific roles and impose a separation of tasks for men and women. Haitian women are responsible for the household and are the only caretakers of children. On the contrary, men are considered to be competent to decide on public matters, including political, economic, and security issues. As a former senator noted: "One cannot think that [a woman] can organize her schedule to be able to participate in political life, and if she does so, one makes her feel guilty—and she also blames herself—because one thinks that this would be time stolen from the family that is her natural and sole environment as well as her main responsibility within the society" (quoted in Manigat 1997, 318).

Because of the social expectation that women are the custodians of the private realm and because Haitian politics is highly corrupt, women are supposed to remain distant from political life and, thus, unspoiled by power and corruption (Almog and Puechguirbal 2007; Puechguirbal, Man, and Loutis 2009). In addition, key obstacles to women's participation in political gatherings, campaigns, and networking are lack of time and financial resources. Representatives of the MINUSTAH Gender Unit interviewed for this study reported that few women in Haiti participate in politics. Data from 1999 show that only 3.5 percent of women were elected as members of Parliament, zero percent as senators, and 4.5 percent as mayors. Only 14 percent of women occupied governmental positions. More recently, out of 102 women who entered the first round of the 2006 legislative elections, only 19 of them made it through the second round. Out of these 19 candidates, 6 were finally elected as members of Parliament and senators (Puechguirbal, Man, and Loutis 2009). Given the limited female presence in the Haitian political arena, new generations of women seeking office inevitably lack female leadership models that could provide examples of political experience, expertise, and management.

As emphasized by representatives of the Ministry for the Status of Women and the MINUSTAH Gender Unit, without access to the public domain and their political rights, women will never be able to enjoy full citizenship, make changes in Haitian society, or improve their personal security. In this regard, the adoption of an affirmative quota will be necessary to encourage women's participation in politics and prominent governmental positions. Specific and ongoing training should also be designed by the Ministry for the Status of Women with the support and collaboration of the UN mission in Haiti. In fact, a pilot project in political couching for Haitian women was organized in 2005 with the support of the MINUSTAH

Gender Unit in anticipation of the 2006 legislative elections. The positive outcome was recounted above.

Community Interventions

The proposed national models for change—through the implementation of legislative measures, the reform of the security forces and the criminal-justice system, and the reinforcement of women's participation in politics—still cannot effectively deliver enduring protection for women or significant improvements in the response to violence without the concurrent adoption of specific interventions at the community level. In this respect, the establishment of and improvement in shelters available to rape victims, including those associated with armed violence, should be an immediate focus. Currently, the few women's shelters operating in Haiti are disproportionately concentrated in Port-au-Prince rather than in the rural and most disadvantaged areas of the country.

Mostly run by women's organizations and solidarity groups, the shelters respond to rape survivors' immediate needs by providing free medical assistance and counseling, testing for and treating sexually transmitted infections, prenatal care for women who become pregnant as a result of rape, as well as medical certificates attesting to the assault and serving as indispensable evidence for pressing charges and prosecuting the case in court. Primarily funded by international donors, among whom Canadians and Americans are the most generous, Haitian shelters often rely on the efforts of survivors, as is the case of KOFAVIV, a women's association founded and led by a group of women from poor neighborhoods in Port-au-Prince who were raped during the military coup of 1991–1994.

However, because of limited resources and the widespread and systematic sexual violence affecting girls and women throughout the country, the number of shelters is inadequate. As mentioned, because shelters are located almost exclusively in Port-au-Prince, girls and women from remote areas of the countryside or inaccessible shantytowns in the capital are unable to benefit from their assistance and support. Because of the long distances involved, the poor system of internal communications, the cost of transportation, as well as the fear of being subjected to further acts of violence or reprisal along the way, victims often either refrain from embarking on the journey or end up reaching the shelters too late to receive preventative treatment for HIV and unwanted pregnancies as well as to verify the fact that forcible sexual intercourse has occurred.

Therefore, although an additional portion of international aid could be devolved to the establishment of new shelters for rape victims, including those associated with armed violence, international organizations already present in the country should implement a capillary system of small structures operating in the rural areas and deprived urban communities in order to provide prompt and effective service to them as well. Informants from MSF confirmed the pressing need for shelters to which survivors of sexual violence may turn for medical assistance and psychological support. Considering the long-term, severe emotional consequences affecting victims of rape, extended post-trauma counseling should also be guaranteed.

Because shelters often are the primary resource for survivors of sexual violence, their provision not only of medical and psychological services but also of adequate legal assistance may ensure that victims receive accurate information about their own rights and the different stages of the judicial process. To date, URAMEL is the only organization in the country that employs such a multilateral approach by requiring rape victims in Port-au-Prince to fill out a basic form about the assault, which may ultimately help in pressing charges. However, so far a similar monitoring system for women associated with armed violence has not been designed in Haiti. Although informants from several national organizations acknowledge that a multilateral strategy of assistance may encourage victims' participation in undertaking collective action against gender-based violence, they also emphasize the critical need to strengthen professional training and capacity building in Haitian medical, psychological, and legal competencies.

A fundamental intervention at the community level aimed at producing long-term solutions requires practical and coordinated prevention strategies. An extensive campaign of sensitization is necessary to inform the public about the prevalence of rape and domestic abuse affecting women in the country, their status as criminal offenses and any relevant consequences, as well as the government's concern about and determination to eradicate the phenomenon. Programs that raise awareness of the incidence, impact, and responses to sexual violence should be conducted in strategic public settings, including schools, under the vigilant supervision of teachers, religious institutions, and recreational centers for youth.

Informants from several civil society associations revealed that one of the major obstacles to overcome is the victims' lack of information about the shelters, services, and resources available to them. Therefore, a sensitization campaign cannot succeed without close collaboration with the mass media, including radio and television as well as flyer coverage in deprived urban communities and remote rural areas. Along the same line, the Ministry for the Status of Women together with the members of the Table de Concertation Nationale have launched a confidential, free telephone hotline service for victims of sexual violence and domestic abuse. Similar initiatives should also be implemented for rape victims associated with the armed groups.

An intense effort should also be made to inject ideas about women's human rights and the prevention of gender-based violence into the public educational curriculum for new generations. Introducing specific modules on sex education in schools may, on the one hand, engender girls' understanding of their own rights and, on the other, raise boys' consciousness of their responsibilities, with the ultimate purpose being to build the basis for future equitable power relationships. Indeed, any long-term strategy for the eradication of gender-based violence and women's violence cannot deliver durable and sustainable change without the active involvement of boys and men. As recommended in a UN report on the role of men and boys in achieving gender equality: "A gender equal society is one that is free of gender-based violence. Involving men and boys is a strategy for creating a non-violent and gender equal society. Men and boys are important agents for changing attitudes, behaviors, and the wider power relations which sustain gender-based violence. Programmes for men against gender-based violence aim at positively influencing both men who oppose violence and those who do not" (United Nations 2003, 32).

However, considering the difficult living conditions, the lack of resources and services, and the widespread street violence, children in the shantytowns are often unable to attend school. Few international and national organizations operating in the conflict areas of Port-au-Prince respond to their needs. In Martissant, in addition to the shelter, KOFAVIV's solidarity group runs the project Kopadim, which provides basic education, peer support groups, and a small microcredit loan program for victims of sexual violence and their children. In Cité Soleil, the international NGO AVSI organizes education, handicrafts, and cosmetology for boys and girls living in the slum, who are often forcibly affiliated with armed groups.

Increasing educational and recreational programs for children in disadvantaged neighborhoods of the capital as well as in remote areas of the countryside is of primary importance. Representatives of MINUSTAH interviewed for this study revealed that the lack of activities and entertainment for youth contributes significantly to the prevalence of gang rapes committed by groups of adolescents, like the Vagabonds. Interestingly, in Cité Soleil during the 2006 World Cup, while boys and men were occupied watching football matches on megascreens endowed by the IOM, the incidence of rape and domestic abuse against girls and women decreased significantly. Education, employment, and activities, therefore, are important tools for engaging boys and men as well as girls and women in alternative and productive occupations and to attaining the ultimate purpose of socializing them toward mutual respect and the condemnation of violence.

The implementation of the practical strategies for intervention proposed in this chapter became even more urgent after the devastating earthquake that struck Haiti on January 12, 2010. The following chapter concludes this book by giving accounts of the struggles and violence that women and girls who survived the disaster are facing on a daily basis in the displacement camps. In addition to the adoption of practical measures to respond promptly to the current situation, a more general understanding of the victimization-offending nexus proposed throughout this book is crucial to free Haitian women and girls long-term from gender-based violence and recruitment by the armed groups. The ultimate goal is to ensure their full participation in rebuilding their communities and their empowerment in the future social fabric.

7

Women in the Aftermath
of the Earthquake

On January 12, 2010, a 7.0-magnitude earthquake struck Haiti, devastating the capital of the country, Port-au Prince, and several other cities. Hundreds of thousands of Haitians died, approximately the same number were injured, and more than a million lost their homes and have been living in the 1,300 displacement camps around the country ever since. Extreme poverty and desperation were coupled with sexual violence affecting the women and girls who survived the natural disaster. The earthquake and its dramatic consequences exacerbated the already arduous conditions for Haitian women and girls as well as violently undermining the precarious capacity and functionality of national institutions, including the government, law enforcement, and the judicial system.

In addition to Port-au-Prince and much of its surrounding countryside, the quake severely affected other areas of the country, including the cities of Petit Goave, Grand Goave, and Leogane in the western part of the country, the town of Jacmel in the South East department, and the town of Miragoane in the Nippes region. Hundreds of thousands of Haitians lost their lives, and about three million people—one-third of Haiti's population—were affected. The United Nations and the Haitian government estimated that the death toll was between 250,000 and 300,000; an equal number of Haitians were injured or permanently disabled, and 1.5 million were left homeless (Cullen and Ivers 2010, 61). More than 600,000 individuals fled Port-au-Prince to safer rural areas and provincial towns such as Gonaives, Saint-Marc, Cap-Haitien, Hince, and Les Cayes, encumbering local communities (Amnesty International 2010, 6). Schools, hospitals, houses, offices, shops, the presidential palace, the cathedral, and the headquarters of the UN mission collapsed.

Seismologists had long warned about the probability of earthquakes on the island of Hispaniola (which comprises Haiti and the Dominican Republic). In fact, the island sits on the Gonaives microplate, a small strip of the earth's crust that compresses the North American and Caribbean tectonic plates. In 1946, the Dominican Republic suffered a severe earthquake, but the 2010 Haitian disaster was more devastating. Its epicenter was just fifteen miles southwest of Port-au-Prince and it began only eight miles below ground, quickly reaching the surface with full force. The shaking was felt as far away as eastern Cuba; a series of powerful aftershocks continued throughout the following few days.

This last chapter examines women's and girls' struggles in the aftermath of the Haitian earthquake. In particular, it focuses on the grievous conditions in the displacement camps, conditions that foster the gender-based violence and abuse that is often perpetrated by members of armed groups or prison escapees. Indeed, the lack of lighting, private sanitary facilities, secure shelters, and police patrolling in the encampment areas endanger women's and girls' safety. The devastation and traumatic loss of family and community members following the earthquake further affect women's resilience and increase their vulnerability to abuse and sexual violence. By examining the conditions and risks faced by women and girls in the displacement camps, this chapter suggests preventive measures and effective responses that international law and humanitarian aid programs should adopt to protect Haitian women and girls from gender-based violence in order to prevent them from engaging in further retaliatory practices.

The Aftermath of the Haitian Earthquake

The country was utterly unequipped to withstand the quake. Most Haitians live in tin-roofed shacks perched on steep ravines that are subject to landslides. In the center of the capital and the neighboring towns, most of the buildings were constructed of inferior concrete and sand without steel rods or any other form of reinforcement. As a result, hillsides packed with slums were swept away by landslides following the quake, as were entire urban neighborhoods. Horrifying mass-media images depicted dead bodies littering the pavement while ambulances swerved among them to rescue those who were still alive and injured. The presidential palace, the Parliament building, the offices of international aid agencies, the Hotel Montana (which housed tourists and foreign delegations) as well as the roof and the aisles of the national cathedral folded like cardboard. The Hotel Christopher, headquarters of the UN peacekeeping mission, collapsed with over two hundred employees trapped inside.

The earthquake severely affected both the capacity and the structure of the Haitian state. Some senators and several other politicians were injured; in addition one third of the country's civil servants died. As a result, the elections that had been scheduled for February 2010 were postponed, and political instability and domestic unrest ensued. In addition to the Parliament and the presidential palace, many other government buildings collapsed or were seriously damaged, including the Supreme Court, the Palace of Justice, ministries, tribunals, and police stations. Over seventy-five police officers perished and hundreds were injured or dispersed. The male prison in Port-au-Prince was destroyed by the earthquake, and about 4,300 prisoners escaped, including some leaders and many members of armed groups. Among the UN personnel, 101 died, including the Special Representative and his deputy, the acting police commissioner, the director of political affairs, the head of the Elections Unit, and many military, police, and civilian officers (United Nations Security Council 2010a).

The international community provided approximately US$9 billion in short- and long-term relief and rebuilding funds. During the first days following the earthquake, emergency relief operations were launched by the United Nations and a number of countries. Canada and the United States deployed thousands of disaster-assistance personnel to the most affected regions of the country. The World Food Program (WFP) provided 3.5 million Haitians with food assistance, including nutrition support for vulnerable groups such as children and pregnant women as well as hospitals and emergency medical organizations. Humanitarian efforts also focused on providing emergency shelter; thousands of tents and tarpaulins were distributed along with basic kitchen and hygiene equipment.

The massive destruction caused by the earthquake forced displaced Haitians to gather spontaneously in camps on every empty piece of land, either public or private, as well as on main roads and squares in urban centers. Amnesty International estimated that about 460 spontaneous settlements sprang up throughout the country within the first few months following the earthquake (2010, 7–8). The Haitian government identified thousands of hectares on the outskirts of Port-au-Prince for temporary relocations and allocated specific sites to host displaced settlements. However, the heavy seasonal rains and the lack of water, sanitation, and hygiene in many spontaneous camps facilitated the spread of cholera, which killed thousands of displaced people by the end of 2010 and the beginning of 2011. The absence of a police force in the camps also contributed to the large number of criminal incidents and armed-group activities as well as the lack of adequate measures aimed at maintaining security and enforcing the law.

Gender-Based Violence in the Displacement Camps

Public attention and humanitarian aid have been focused primarily on rebuilding efforts and meeting basic needs. However, given the increasing insecurity and gang activity in the makeshift camps for the displaced, along with the escape of prisoners, women and girls have been daily victims of sexual violence and exploitation (Associated Press in Port-au-Prince 2010). Many settlements are overcrowded and lack safe accommodations and adequate sanitary facilities to allow women and girls proper privacy. Serious shortcomings in lighting the camps also make women and girls vulnerable to aggression and violence at night (Amnesty International 2010, 11). Data collected through a survey of households in four camps for internally displaced persons in and around the capital reveal that 14 percent of the respondents declared that, since the earthquake, one or more members of their household have been victimized by sexual violence. Among the victims, 86 percent were women and girls, and 14 percent were men and boys. Incidents of sexual violence have occurred both during the day and at night mostly when the victims were inside their shelters or on their way to obtain water. According to the same study, about 70 percent of the respondents admitted being more concerned about sexual violence after the earthquake than before (Center for Human Rights and Global Justice, NYU School of Law 2011).

Such data reflect the well-documented evidence that gender-based violence typically increases in postdisaster settings, in which the infrastructure is damaged and unsafe, living conditions are poor, and the security services are inadequate. Indeed, in the aftermath of Hurricane Katrina, incidents of sexual violence against women, and especially intimate-partner violence, tripled (Anastario, Shehab, and Lawry 2009). Similarly, a substantial increase in gender-based violence, particularly domestic violence, and gender inequalities was registered after the South Asian tsunami of 2004 (Ariyabandu 2006; Pittaway, Bartolomei, and Rees 2007).

In September 2010, the United Nations described the vulnerability of children and women and the scale of sexual violence perpetrated, especially in the camps neighboring the large slums of Cité Soleil and Martissant, where several armed groups operate (United Nations Security Council 2010b, 3). Nevertheless, the report acknowledged that the lack of accurate and aggregated data on gender-based violence makes it difficult to assess the true extent of the increase of sexual violence in Haiti since the earthquake. A study conducted in Parc Jean Marie Vincent, a spontaneous camp in Port-au-Prince, revealed that although the United Nations and the PNH regularly patrolled the area, most of the respondents still felt unsafe (Cullen and Ivers 2010). In particular, incidents of sexual violence were reported against women and girls who had been assaulted on their way to obtain water at night. A young victim recounted:

> My mother is dead, my father is dead. I made a small shelter on Place Petion in Champ de Mars to live in. . . . I'm living alone. I had a tarpaulin but it was torn down and M. gave me a small tent to live in. . . . On 16 February, I went out to buy some water at around 8 P.M. When I came back to my home, I lay down. A man came in. He removed the sheets covering me and when I tried to cry he put his hand over my mouth. . . . He tore off my underwear and raped me. He kicked me and punched me before leaving. When I was able to call for help, he cut through the tarpaulin and fled. . . . On 17 February I went to the General Hospital. . . . I lost a lot of blood. I bled for twenty-two days. . . . At the hospital there was a foreign doctor.

He gave me some pills and asked me to return again because I was wounded. He gave me pills to fight infection and HIV/AIDS. He told me I should eat when taking the medicine. . . . I didn't have any money to buy food. (Amnesty International 2011, 12)

The lack of separate sanitary facilities for men and women also was pinpointed as a danger for women's personal security (United Nations Stabilization Mission in Haiti, Human Rights Section 2010). Furthermore, in the relief camp of Delmas 14, girls reported being scared of going to the latrines at night because of the absence of adequate lighting. Another victim shared her tragic story:

At around 9 P.M. on 3 May, I left my tent to go to the toilet [one of the plastic toilets near the Presidential Palace]. While I was in the toilet, the door opened—there was no catch to lock the door. At first I thought it was the wind, but in fact it was a man who opened the door. It was dark. There were two men: one came into the toilet, the other stayed outside as lookout. I tried to fight the man who came in, but he pulled a knife and pressed into my groin. After he'd raped me, he ran away. I called out for help immediately and a police car patrolling the area stopped. I explained to the police officers what had happened. They asked me where the attackers were, but when I told them that they ran away, the officers told me there was nothing they could do. (Amnesty International 2011, 14)

Data from a study conducted in the shantytown of Cité Soleil showed that rape and other forms of violence, including robbery, beating, and fighting, are rampant in the encampment areas (Institute Interuniversitaire de Recherche et de Developpment 2010). Many women and girls reported having been beaten by men out of rage. Respondents acknowledged that sexual violence was widespread where they were living, and, in some cases, they had personally witnessed or experienced violent attacks. Accounts from informants in the Institute Interuniversitaire study declared that in Cité Soleil the armed groups manage to obtain food aid and shelter. Girls are often obliged to trade sex in order to secure food and refuge from the heavy rains. According to respondents, sexual assaults and the exploitation of girls usually occur at night, when police forces have left the relief camps and the gangs take control of the territory. More than 60 percent of the participants in the study believed that women and children are less protected and safe in the camps than in the shanties where they lived before the earthquake.

A survey of Port-au-Prince households conducted in March 2010 estimated that 3 percent of the individuals living in the capital had been victims of sexual violence in the first two months following the earthquake (Kolbe et al. 2010). MSF reported treating 212 victims of rape in the five months after the tragedy (Médecins sans Frontières 2010). SOFA documented 718 cases of gender-based violence in its clinics between January and June 2010 (SOFA 2010). KOFAVIV documented the stories of some of its patients. One of them reported:

> I am nineteen years old. Prior to the earthquake, I lived in Carrefour Feuille. I am now staying in a camp in Martissant with my aunt, her children, and my four-year-old daughter. We no longer have access to adequate shelter; therefore, we are sleeping under sheets. On January 20, 2010, we heard gunshots fired in the camp. Shortly thereafter, around 9 P.M., nine men entered our sheltered area. Four of these men stayed behind with my aunt and brutally abused her. The other five abducted me and kept me somewhere for two days. During this time, the five men repeatedly beat and raped me. I was not sure if they were going to kill me and if I would ever be allowed to return to my family. Thankfully, they released me after those two days. Although I suffered greatly and was wounded on my mouth, I could not afford to go to the doctor. I feel extremely depressed and helpless. I was afraid to go to the police because of what those men did to me, so I did not report my attack. I knew the police would do nothing to protect us. We have no way to protect ourselves from such brutality, and each day and every day I am fearful that those men will come back again.[1]

On August 2010, another young woman supported by KOFAVIV was kidnapped by five armed men who dragged her into a truck and raped her. In July 2010, a nineteen-year-old woman was assaulted by three men when she left her tent to use the latrine during the night. Only a few days later, another victim was raped by a man who broke into her tent in the middle of the night, threatening her with a machete and a gun. And a five-year-old girl was brutally raped and suffered bleeding from vaginal tearing and severe consequences of an infection. KOFAVIV reported that, unfortunately, her grandmother was not able to buy the medications prescribed by the doctor.[2]

According to another study, most victims reported being raped by more than one individual who was unknown to them and usually armed with guns, machetes, or other weapons. Many of the survivors declared that they would not be able to identify their assailants because the rapes often occurred at night, the perpetrators were wearing masks, and the emotional shock of the assault impaired their recollection of the events. Some victims, however, were able to identify their attackers as members of armed groups or fugitives from prison. They reported being raped mostly at night between 9 P.M. and 3 A.M., although some attacks also occurred during the day. Women were attacked inside the relief camps in their tents, in the latrines, or in the middle of the street. Sometimes, perpetrators cut the tent with a knife to gain access to their shelters. One woman reported being kidnapped from her camp and taken to a house where she was beaten and gang raped repeatedly for several days until she managed to escape (Institute for Justice and Democracy in Haiti et al. 2010, 11).

Further testimonies revealed that the earthquake destroyed Haitian women's social support networks, thus increasing their vulnerability to violence. Many of them lost their husbands and have been left with the primary responsibility of providing care and financial support for children, the elderly, and the newly disabled people (Institute for Justice and Democracy in Haiti et al. 2010, 11). According to people interviewed for my study, prior to the earthquake, the majority of Haitian women worked as merchants in the market, but many of them lost their goods under the rubble. Extreme poverty and the traumatic loss of family or community members hamper their resilience and shape their decisions about where to live, thus increasing their vulnerability to sexual violence and recruitment by armed groups.

International Legal Instruments

The primary areas of international law that can provide protection to women affected by natural disasters are international humanitarian law, international human-rights law, and international disaster-response law. Addressing women' struggles and, specifically, gender-based violence in postdisaster settings is challenging for countries like Haiti that already face extreme poverty, armed violence, and poor governance. Public attention and the international community have necessarily been focused on rebuilding efforts and meeting basic needs. However, given the increasing economic and physical vulnerability of displaced women and girls, an international-law response also becomes crucially important in addressing gender-based violence and designing adequate relief measures for victims.

Traditionally, international humanitarian law focuses on civilian violations perpetrated in armed conflicts, including gender-based violence. However, as previously discussed in this book, the provisions of humanitarian law have also been applied in the context of armed violence and thus, by analogy, can be used to address sexual violence against women perpetrated by armed groups in the displacement camps. Moreover, the destruction and breakdown of the society as well as the wretched living conditions following a natural disaster closely resemble the situation experienced by endangered civilians in wartime. Therefore, international humanitarian norms could be applied to protect women and girls from rape and sexual assaults in the aftermath of the Haitian earthquake.

In addition to humanitarian law, several instruments of international human-rights law aim specifically to protect the rights of women and girls in postdisaster settings. Although international human-rights law definitely applies to violations against women in postdisaster settings, important limitations hamper its effectiveness when it comes to enforcing economic, social, and cultural rights. Indeed, under international law states' obligations to adopt adequate measures toward the realization of economic, social, and cultural rights are based on the maximum extent of their available resources. But the devastation caused by the earthquake has exhausted Haiti's already scarce resources, leaving little hope for the implementation of reforms and programs aimed at protecting women and girls from gender-based violence. However, international human-rights law urges other countries to cooperate in assisting states affected by natural disasters.

Other international-law standards that can be used to address women's rights in postdisaster settings are the recommendations contained in the United Nations Guiding Principles on Internal Displacement (United Nations Office for the Coordination of Humanitarian Affairs 1998; see also United Nations High Commissioner for Refugees 2003). Based on international humanitarian and human-rights law and analogous refugee law, the Guiding Principles aim to protect internally displaced individuals in situations of internal conflict, natural disasters, and forced displacement. They are designed to serve as a guide for governments, international organizations, and all other relevant actors in providing assistance and protection to internally displaced people. For instance, Principle 11 states that internally displaced persons shall be protected in particular against rape, torture, cruel, inhuman, or degrading treatment or punishment, as well as other outrages upon personal dignity such as acts of gender-specific violence. Indeed, the Guiding Principles acknowledge that because displaced women and girls are removed from their home communities, they become particularly vulnerable to rape, sexual exploitation, forced prostitution, and slavery (United Nations Office for the Coordination of Humanitarian Affairs 2000).

Finally, emerging international disaster-response law includes a number of recommendations aimed at improving the lives of vulnerable and displaced people by mobilizing the international community to respond to disasters that exceed local and national capacities. Based on the Guidelines for the Domestic Facilitation and Regulation of International Disaster Relief and Initial Recovery Assistance (International Federation of the Red Cross and Red Crescent Societies 2007), international disaster-response law promotes cooperation and coordination among states and international organizations in response to disasters. It also fosters the development of the capacity of national associations to engage with governments on issues concerning the protection of the rights of persons living in post-disaster settings. Specifically, the Guidelines clarify the responsibilities of states for planning, organizing, and managing disaster relief operations.

The primary limitation of the three bodies of law applicable to displaced women and girls in natural disasters is the lack of enforcement of their provisions. Indeed, regardless of the binding nature of international humanitarian and human-rights treaties addressing gender-based violence, states often fail to comply with their obligations to adopt and implement adequate legislation and related measures. Similarly, the multiple

UN resolutions on women, peace, and security, the Guiding Principles on Internal Displacement, as well as the Guidelines for the Domestic Facilitation and Regulation of International Disaster Relief and Initial Recovery Assistance are not effectively applied, not so much because of their legally nonbinding nature as because the affected states lack the necessary resources to implement them.

However, over the years, international law has attempted to mitigate such shortcomings by recognizing that governments have positive obligations to exercise due diligence to prevent, investigate, and punish acts of violence against women, whether those acts are perpetrated by the state or by private individuals or organizations. Governments also have the duty to adopt and revise domestic legislation for the protection of women as well as to provide access to just and effective remedies and specialized assistance to victims of violence, including vulnerable women living in internal displacement camps. A fundamental principle connected to the application of the due diligence standard is that of nondiscrimination, which means that states are required to show the same level of commitment to preventing, investigating, punishing, and providing remedies for gender-based violence as they show in relation to other forms of violence.

The due diligence standard has paved the way for recognition of violence against women as a human-rights violation as well as for a new understanding of the doctrine of state responsibility, according to which states can be held accountable for gender-based violence, regardless of whether the perpetrator is a public or a private actor. Accordingly, Article 9 of the Convention of Belém do Pará, for instance, sets forth that States Parties shall take special account of the vulnerability of women to violence because of their status as migrants, refugees, or displaced persons (art. 9), among other reasons. Similarly, the CEDAW General Recommendation No. 19 recognizes states' liability for private actions if they fail to act with due diligence to prevent violations of rights or to investigate and punish acts of violence, or to provide compensation to victims (art. 9).

In 1999, the United Nations Special Rapporteur on violence against women developed criteria for assessing state compliance with obligations of due diligence; the list included the ratification of international human-rights instruments; constitutional guarantees of equality for women; the existence of national legislation and/or administrative sanctions providing adequate redress for women victims of violence; policies or plans of action for dealing with violence against women; the gender-sensitivity of the criminal justice system and police; and the accessibility and availability of support services for victims (United Nations Economic and Social Council, Commission on Human Rights 2006, 57). Therefore, under international law, the primary responsibility to comply with positive obligations to pro-. tect women from gender-based violence falls on the individual state. However, in the case of states affected by a natural disaster, like Haiti, where devastation impairs the government's ability to perform its functions, foreign states and international organizations are called on to cooperate and to coordinate relief efforts for victims of violence.

Responses to Women's Struggles in the Displacement Camps

Studies conducted in the encampment areas have shown that preventive measures should be taken to preclude the occurrence of gender-based violence as well as to alleviate the struggles of women and girls living in the aftermath of the earthquake. Primary efforts should be to provide adequate lighting throughout the camps, private sanitary and bathing facilities, and shelters or other secure living accommodations. Waterproof and fire-resistant plastic tents that have been used as an immediate housing response should be replaced by transitional shelters that combine some emergency supplies with more robust building materials, including cement and steel roof panels (United States Agency for International Development 2010). An infrastructure redevelopment program should then follow to rebuild communities in the areas affected by the earthquake; to guarantee that such communities have access to clean water, sewage, and electricity; and to create job opportunities for women to promote their participation in the economic development of Haiti.

Data collected by civil society organizations revealed that many victims do not receive medical care after the attacks because of a lack of information, long waits, the impossibility of paying for transportation to reach the services, and fear of stigmatization (Institute for Justice and Democracy in Haiti et al. 2010, 12). However, the few functioning clinics are overwhelmed with patients and struggle to adequately meet the demand for health care resulting from the assaults. Thus, prompt interventions should be made to open additional medical centers equipped with HIV prophylaxis and emergency contraception as well as to increase the number of female providers assisting rape victims. Comprehensive information regarding the location of medical services and the fact that they are available free of charge should also be provided in displacement camps. Moreover, free medical certificates should be issued to victims of sexual violence to document the assault in a criminal trial. Finally, the number of psychiatrists and trauma specialists should be increased to provide psychological assistance to the many rape victims who are suffering from depression and post-traumatic stress disorders.

As revealed by this study, women and girls seldom report incidents of sexual violence to the authorities because of the lack of police response, the distrust of the justice system, and the fear of retaliation and stigmatization in their communities. Civil society organizations have reported that the PNH rarely patrol in the displacement camps, and the police stations that are still operational employ few female officers and lack safe and confidential facilities that would allow victims to lodge their complaints (Amnesty International 2010). The fear of retaliation by the perpetrators, who often live in the same displacement camp, as well as social stigmatization within local communities are intimidating factors for rape victims. Indeed, women have reported being threatened with further harm or death if they tell anyone about an attack.

Police corruption and inefficiency are also rampant. Grassroots organizations reported the case of a victim who had approached the police to file a complaint and was asked to buy them gas for their car (Institute for Justice and Democracy in Haiti et al. 2010, 14). Once the woman gave them the money, the police refused to drive to the nearby camp and investigate the crime. Other examples include women who approached the police for help and received the response that "there was nothing they could do," that the assault was not a responsibility of the police but rather of the Haiti's president, Préval, and that the victims "should return when [they] had identified and/or captured [their] attackers."

In addition to attempts to decrease corruption and inefficiency, adequate patrolling should be carried out in and around the camps. Police stations should guarantee a safe and private space for rape victims to lodge their complaints. In addition, more female security guards should be recruited to assist women and girls in reporting sexual assaults, thus mini-mizing the mockery, shame, and stigma experienced by rape survivors. Similarly, additional protection and access to justice should be guaranteed to victims of sexual violence. In the Haitian judicial system there is no state-funded legal aid or witness protection available for rape survivors. Only a few civil society organizations provide services that encourage vic-tims to report the assaults and accompany and represent them through the legal process. However, severely affected by the earthquake in their capacity and infrastructure facilities, such organizations struggle to keep up with the overwhelming number of assaults.

Representatives of these organizations have denounced the many unpunished rape cases in Haiti since the earthquake. According to them, the Haitian government has just begun to prosecute a small number of them. Indeed, when the police have arrested the alleged perpetrators, suspects have been often released because of poor investigations and the bribery of prosecutors by the defendants or their families.[3] Thus, imme-diate action should be taken to end the widespread climate of impunity across the enforcement and justice systems; such impunity is a consid-erable disincentive for victims to report assaults. In addition, adequate training should be provided to police and justice officers responsible for addressing sexual violence and assisting rape survivors. Finally, women and girls, and particularly grassroots organizations, should be guaranteed full participation in the relief efforts, especially in addressing gender-based violence and women's struggles in the displacement camps.

The discussion throughout this book has made clear the influences that violence against women, and particularly sexual harm, might have in the decision-making processes of the victims. Specifically, the discussion has contributed insights into the conditions and incentives that motivate rape victims to join the armed groups in Haiti and to become involved in crimi-nal and community violence. The data, drawn from in-depth interviews, focus-group sessions, and participant observation with female victims and perpetrators of violence and with representatives of international and national institutions and civil society organizations working on the research topic suggest the intense correlation between gender-based and women's violence in the metropolitan slum communities of Haiti.

An ultimate understanding of the conditions and incentives that motivate women to become involved with armed groups depends on analyzing the various ways in which violence is intertwined with poverty and gender inequality in Haitian cultural and social settings. The analysis of the data revealed three main categories of motivation for women and girls to engage in criminal and community violence. In particular, adult women reported having been chiefly driven to associate with armed factions either by a need to protect themselves and their families or by their rage against state negligence and ineffective law enforcement. Girls, however, reported being more prone to join the gangs to attain social status and respect within their own communities and to retaliate against their past of sexual abuse and stigmatization.

Although these motivations might often overlap and cannot totally encompass the complexity of the victimization-offending nexus, they deepen the understanding of the diverse incentives women might have at different stages of their lives as well as the context within which female violence is rooted. Either because of their need for protection or because of their anger and craving for social revenge, women engage in violence as a way of responding to and resisting the cumulative ordeals of deprivation, denial, and sexual harm. As in other contexts, these living experiences critically shape women's choices and strategies for adaptation, work, resilience, and coping behaviors (Boyden 1994; Wesely 2006).

Ultimately, this investigation leads to questioning whether, or at least to what extent, female aggression committed within a context of armed violence should be understood as "an extremely practical survival mechanism" (Boyden 1994, 263) or as a conscious decision. Important implications ensue from the answers to such a question, ultimately charging international and national legal institutions with the challenging duty of devising fair and adequate responses. To date, despite the international commitments undertaken by the Haitian government and the efforts made by the national legislature to comply with international human-rights standards, security and justice responses to gender-based violence and women's violence remain inadequate.

Strategies for action, legal measures, and policy recommendations proposed in this book are intended to stimulate a new and sensitive debate about gender-based violence and women's violence in Haiti as well as to suggest more effective measures to guarantee their protection. International humanitarian law and human-rights law should adopt specific programs, along the lines of those implemented in other countries affected by armed conflict, in order to rehabilitate and reintegrate women and girls in the Haitian society. Further measures at the national, political, and community level are also suggested throughout the book to promote a cooperative and multilateral approach toward both women's victimization and their retaliation. On a broader scale, solutions for the structural causes of both violence against women and women's violence depend largely on increasing their educational level and implementing effective measures aimed at strengthening their personal, social, and economic empowerment.

After the earthquake that severely affected Haiti in 2010, identifying effective responses for root causes of gender-based violence has become ever more urgent. Indeed, the analysis above has documented that, in the midst of desperation and disarray, because of their increasing economic and physical vulnerability, women and girls have been daily victims of rape in the makeshift camps for the displaced. A further assessment of whether and to what extent the tragedy will lead to changing patterns of violence against women as well as their motivations to retaliate will be much needed in years to come. Meanwhile, as suggested by this book, international law and humanitarian aid can help in providing effective measures to improve women's and girls' living conditions as well as in protecting them from violence and recruitment by the armed groups. Further relief efforts should be directed toward funding adequate programs and interventions to reintegrate women and girls in postdisaster communities and to encourage their active participation in rebuilding a more peaceful country.

NOTES

INTRODUCTION

1. Haitian proverb.
2. Established in 1997, the Ombudsman's mandate is to protect all citizens from violations by government officials. Most of the cases submitted to the Ombudsman are allegations of police brutality, including sexual violence against girls and women.
3. Restavèks are children who are sent by their parents to work for host households as domestic servants because the parents lack resources to support them; the term usually refers specifically to children who are abused.

CHAPTER 1   GENDER-BASED VIOLENCE AND WOMEN'S VIOLENCE IN CONTEXT

1. United Nations Security Council, Resolution 940 (31 July 1994), S/RES/940 (1994), authorizing the formation of a multinational force to restore the legitimately elected president and authorities of the government of Haiti and extending the mandate of the UN mission in Haiti.
2. United Nations Security Council, Resolution 1542 (30 April 2004), S/RES/1542 (2004). establishing MINUSTAH and defining its mandate.
3. United Nations Security Council, Resolution 1702 (15 August 2006), S/RES/1702 (2006).

CHAPTER 2   GENDER-BASED VIOLENCE IN HAITI

1. Haitian currency: 1.00 Haitian *gourde* is equivalent to US$0.02.

CHAPTER 3   UNDERSTANDING WOMEN'S VIOLENCE IN HAITI

1. For studies on male aggression, see, generally, Coie and Dodge 2006; Maccoby and Jacklin 1974. For women's natural hostility to violence, see, generally, Tiger 1969; Tiger and Fox 1970. For women's socialization to that hostility, see, generally, Block 1984; Campbell 1984; Steffensmeier and Allan 1991, 67–93. For more recent studies, see also Alison 2004; Sharlah 1999.

2. For the comparison of females to their male peers, see, generally, Adler 1975; Figueira-McDonough 1989; Rhodes and Fischer 1993. For contextualization of female aggression, see, generally, Chesney-Lind 1989; Daly and Maher 1998; Gilfus 1992; Heidensohn 1985.

3. See Baker-Miller 1976; Chodorow 1978; Gilligan 1982. See also Belknap 1996; Chesney-Lind 1989; Heidensohn 1985.

4. For a general classifications of armed groups in Haiti, see United Nations Stabilization Mission in Haiti and United Nations Development Programme in Haiti 2006. See also United Nations General Assembly/Security Council 2006; and Puechguirbal, Man, and Loutis 2009.

CHAPTER 4   LEGAL FRAMEWORKS

1. Charter of the United Nations, art. 1(3). Other references in the Charter to non-discrimination on the basis of sex are included in arts. 13, 55(c), and 76(c).

2. States Parties are the states that have ratified the treaty and, therefore, are bound by the relevant provisions.

3. United Nations, General Recommendation No. 12, Committee on the Elimination of Discrimination Against Women, U.N. Doc. A/44/38 at 75, 1989.

4. United Nations, General Recommendation No. 19, Committee on the Elimination of Discrimination Against Women, U.N. Doc. A/47/38, 1992.

5. United Nations, Declaration on the Elimination of Violence Against Women, adopted 20 December 1993, G.A. Res. 48/104, U.N. GAOR, 48th Sess., 85th plen. mtg., U.N. Doc. A/RES/48/104 (1993).

6. The mandate of the Special Rapporteur on violence against women, its causes and consequences, was established by the Commission on Human Rights in 1994 (Commission on Human Rights resolution 1994/45) and was extended in 1997, 2000, 2003, and 2011 (Commission on Human Rights resolutions 1997/44, 2000/45, 2003/45 and Human Rights Council resolution 16/7, respectively).

7. United Nations, Optional Protocol to the Convention on the Elimination of All Forms of Discrimination against Women, adopted 2000, G.A. Res. 4, U.N. GAOR, 54th Sess., Supp. No. 49, U.N. Doc. A/RES/54/4 (1999) (entered into force 22 December 2000).

8. Inter-American Convention on the Prevention, Punishment, and Eradication of Violence Against Women. Adopted 9 June 1994, entered into force March 5, 1995, 33 I.L.M. 1534, 1994.

9. United Nations, Convention on the Rights of the Child, adopted 20 November 1989, G.A. Res. 44/25, U.N. GAOR 44th Sess., Supp. No. 49, U.N. Doc. A/44/49 (1989), entered into force 2 September 1990.

10. United Nations Security Council, Resolution 1539 of 22 April 2004, S/RES/1539 (2004).

11. United Nations Security Council, Resolution 1325 of 31 October 2000, S/RES/1325 (2000).

12. United Nations Security Council, Resolution 1743 of 15 February 2007, S/RES/1743 (2007); United Nations Security Council, Resolution 1780 of 15 October 2007,

S/RES/1780 (2007); United Nations Security Council, Resolution 1840 of 14 October 2008, S/RES/1840 (2008).

13. Protocol Additional to the Geneva Conventions of 12 August 1949, and relating to the Protection of Victims of International Armed Conflict (Protocol I), 8 June 1977; Protocol Additional to the Geneva Conventions of 12 August 1949, and relating to the Protection of Victims of Non-International Armed Conflict (Protocol II), 8 June 1977.

14. United Nations, Optional Protocol to the Convention on the Rights of the Child on the Involvement of Children in Armed Conflict, adopted 25 May 2000, G.A. Res. A/RES/54/263 (entered into force 12 February 2002).

15. United Nations Security Council, Resolution 820 of 17 April 1993, S/RES/820 (1993).

16. Trial Chamber I, Review of Indictment pursuant to Rule 61, *Prosecutor v. Karadzic and Mladic*, Cases Nos. IT-95-5-R61 and IT-95-18-R61, 11 July 1996.

17. Renée Guisan, member of the ICRC, statement to the Fourth World Conference on Women (United Nations 1995).

18. United Nations Security Council, Resolution 1820 of 19 June 2008, S/RES/1820 (2008); United Nations Security Council, Resolution 1888 of 30 September 2009, S/RES/1888 (2009); United Nations Security Council, Resolution 1889 of 5 October 2009, S/RES/1889 (2009).

CHAPTER 5   VICTIMS' HELP-SEEKING AND THE CRIMINAL-JUSTICE RESPONSE

1. The Table de Concertation Nationale sur les Violences Faites aux Femmes is a coordination network comprised of the following partners: the Ministry for the Status of Women, the Ministry of Justice, the Ministry of Public Health, several civil society institutions—National Coordination for Advocacy of Women's Rights (KONAP), URAMEL, GHESKIO, Médecins du Monde (MDM), and Caritas—and UN agencies—UNFPA, UNDP, WHO, and MINUSTAH. The Table de Concertation Nationale is composed of three technical commissions: (i) Commission de Collecte des Données, responsible for the standardization of the process and the intervention; (ii) Commission de Prise en Charge, responsible for the production of standardized forms and guidelines; and (iii) Commission de Prévention et Sensibilisation, responsible for the establishment of a coordinated response.

CHAPTER 6   STRATEGIES FOR ACTION

1. Convention against Torture and Other Cruel, Inhuman, or Degrading Treatment or Punishment, adopted 10 December 1984, G.A. Res. A/RES/39/46 (entered into force 26 June 1987); Inter-American Convention to Prevent and Punish Torture, adopted 9 December 1985, OEA/Ser. L.V./II 82 doc.6 rev.1 at 83 (1992) (entered into force 28 February 1987).

2. United Nations, Optional Protocol to the Convention on the Rights of the Child on the Involvement of Children in Armed Conflict, adopted 25 May 2000,

G.A. Res. A/RES/54/263 (entered into force 12 February 2002); United Nations, Optional Protocol to the Convention on the Rights of the Child on the Sale of Children, Child Prostitution, and Child Pornography, adopted 25 May 2000, G.A. Res. A/RES/54/263 (entered into force 18 January 2002).

3. United Nations Security Council, Resolution 1325 of 31 October 2000, S/RES/1325 (2000).

4. United Nations, Convention on the Rights of the Child, adopted 20 November 1989, G.A. Res. 44/25, U.N. GAOR 44th Sess., Supp. No. 49, U.N. Doc. A/44/49 1989 (entered into force 2 September 1990).

5. National Commission for Disarmament, Demobilization, and Reintegration (CNDDR), National Strategy for Disarmament, Violence Reduction, and Community Security, adopted December 2006, Port-au-Prince.

CHAPTER 7   WOMEN IN THE AFTERMATH OF THE EARTHQUAKE

1. Request by the International Women's Human Rights Clinic at the City University of New York School of Law et al. to the Honorable Members of the Inter-American Commission on Human Rights, Organization of American States (OAS), December 22, 2010, Appendix A—Petitioner Declarations.

2. Republic of Haiti Submission to the United Nations Universal Periodic Review, 12th Session of the Working Group on the UPR Human Rights Council, Gender-Based Violence against Haitian Women and Girls in Internal Displacement Camps, October 3–14, 2011, 3.

3. Ibid., 4.

REFERENCES

Acoca, L., and K. Dedel. 1998. *No Place to Hide: Understanding and Meeting the Needs of Girls in the California Juvenile Justice System.* San Francisco: National Council on Crime and Delinquency.

Adler, Freda. 1975. *Sisters in Crime.* New York: McGraw-Hill.

Alison, Miranda. 2004. "Women as Agents of Political Violence: Gendering Security." *Security Dialogue* 35 (4): 447–463.

Almog, Nava, and Nadine Puechguirbal. 2007. *Une ville dans le sable—Femmes en politique pour changer Haiti: L'histoire du Programme de Coaching pour un Nouveau Leadership* [A city in the sand—Women in politics to change Haiti: History of the Coaching Program for a New Leadership]. Port-au-Prince: Authors.

Altman, Dennis. 2001. *Global Sex.* Chicago: University of Chicago Press.

American Correctional Association. 1990. *The Female Offender: What Does the Future Hold?* Washington, DC: St. Mary's Press.

Amnesty International. 2010. *Haiti: After the Earthquake, Initial Mission Findings.* March. http://www.amnesty.org/en/library/info/AMR36/004/2010.

———. 2011. *Aftershocks: Women Speak Out against Sexual Violence in Haiti's Camps.* AMR 36/001/2011. January. http://www.amnesty.org/en/library/info/AMR36/001/2011.

Anastario, Michael, Nadine Shehab, and Lynn Lawry. 2009. "Increased Gender-Based Violence among Women Internally Displaced in Mississippi Two Years Post-Hurricane Katrina." *Disaster Medical and Public Health Preparedness* 3 (1): 18–26.

Ariyabandu, Madhavi M. 2006. "Gender Issues in Recovery from the December 2004 Indian Ocean Tsunami: The Case of Sri Lanka." *Earthquake Spectra* 20: 759–775.

Associated Press in Port-au-Prince. 2010. "Rape Rampant in Haiti's Earthquake Camps." March 17. http://www.cbsnews.com/2100-202_162-6306562.html.

Baker, M. Ahmad. 1991. "Psychological Response of Palestinian Children to Environmental Stress Associated with Military Occupation." *Journal of Refugee Studies* 4 (3): 237–247.

Baker-Miller, Jean. 1976. *Toward a New Psychology of Women.* Boston: Beacon Press.

Ballard, R. John, and John J. Sheehan. 1998. *Upholding Democracy: The United States Military Campaign in Haiti, 1994–1997.* Westport, CT: Praeger.

Bartlett, Katharine T., and Deborah L. Rhode. 2006. *Gender and Law: Theory, Doctrine, Commentary.* 4th ed. New York: Aspen.

Belknap, Joanne. 1996. *The Invisible Woman: Gender, Crime, and Justice.* Belmont, MA: Wadsworth.

Bell, Beverly. 2001. *Walking on Fire: Haitian Women's Stories of Survival and Resistance.* Ithaca, NY: Cornell University Press.

Bernard, J. B., G. de Zalduondo, M. L. Mayard, N. Phelle, E. St. Louis, M. Saint Louis, and R. Abellard. 1993. "L'insalubrité dans les bidonvilles: Le cas de Cité-Soleil" [Insalubrity in the slums: The case of Cité-Soleil]. Paper presented at the meeting of the Association of American Anthropologists, Washington, DC, November.

Block, Jeanne. 1984. *Sex Role Identity and Ego Development.* San Francisco: Jossey-Bass.

Boyden, Jo. 1994. "Children's Experience of Conflict Related Emergencies: Some Implications for Relief Policy and Practice." *Disasters* 18 (3): 254–267.

Brownmiller, Susan. 1975. *Against Our Will: Men, Women, and Rape.* New York: Simon & Schuster.

———. 1994. *Making Female Bodies the Battlefield in Mass Rape: The War against Women in Bosnia Herzegovina.* Lincoln: University of Nebraska Press.

Byrnes, Andrew. 1995. "The Committee on the Elimination of Discrimination against Women." In *The United Nations and Human Rights: A Critical Appraisal,* edited by Philip Alston. Oxford: Oxford University Press.

Cadet, Jean-Robert. 1998. *Restavec: From Haitian Slave Child to Middle-Class American.* Austin: Texas University Press.

Cairns, Ed. 1996. *Children and Political Violence.* Oxford: Blackwell.

Campbell, Anne. 1984. *The Girls in the Gang.* New York: Blackwell.

Center for Human Rights and Global Justice, NYU School of Law. 2011. *Sexual Violence in Haiti's IDP Camps: Results of a Household Survey.* March. New York: Center for Human Rights and Global Justice, NYU School of Law.

Centre Haïtien de Recherches et d'Actions pour la Promotion Féminine (CHREPROF). 1996. *Violences exercées sur les femmes et les filles en Haïti* [Forms of violence performed against women and girls in Haiti]. November. Port-au-Prince, Haiti: Centre Haïtien de Recherches et d'Actions pour la Promotion Féminine.

Charlesworth, Hilary, and Christine Chinkin. 2000. *The Boundaries of International Law: A Feminist Analysis.* Huntington, NY: Juris.

Chesney-Lind, Meda. 1989. "Girls' Crime and Woman's Place: Toward a Feminist Model of Female Delinquency." *Crime & Delinquency* 35: 5–29.

Chinkin, Christine. 1994. "Rape and Sexual Abuse of Women in International Law." Symposium on the Yugoslav Crisis: New International Law Issues. *European Journal of International Law* 5: 326–341.

Chodorow, Nancy. 1978. *The Reproduction of Mothering: Psychoanalysis and the Sociology of Gender.* Berkeley: University of California Press.

Coie, J. D., and K. A. Dodge. 2006. "Aggression and Antisocial Behavior." In *Handbook of Child Psychology,* vol. 3, *Social, Emotional, and Personality Development,* edited by N. Eisenberg. Hoboken, NJ: Wiley.

Coomaraswamy, Radhika. 2005. "The Varied Contours of Violence against Women in South Asia." Paper presented at the Fifth South Asia Regional Ministerial Conference, Celebrating Beijing + 10, Islamabad, Pakistan, May 3–5.

Council of Europe. 2004. *Gender Mainstreaming*. http://www.gendermainstreaming -planungstool.at/_lccms_/downloadarchive/00003/Europarat.pdf.

Cullen, Kimberly A., and Louise C. Ivers. 2010. "Human Rights Assessment in Parc Jean Marie Vincent, Port-au-Prince, Haiti." *Health and Human Rights in Practice* 12 (2): 61–72.

Daly, Kathleen, and Lisa Maher. 1998. *Criminology at the Crossroads: Feminist Readings in Crime and Justice*. New York: Oxford University Press.

Deibert, Michael. 2006. *Notes from the Last Testament: The Struggle for Haiti*. New York: Seven Stories Press.

Dubois, Laurent. 2012. *Haiti: The Aftershocks of History*. New York: Metropolitan Books.

Enloe, Cynthia. 2002. "Demilitarization—or More of the Same? Feminist Questions to Ask in the Post-war Moment." In *The Post-war Moment: Militaries, Masculinities, and International Peacekeeping*, edited by C. Cockburn, and D. Zarkov, 22–32. London: Lawrence & Wishart.

Faedi, Benedetta. 2008. "The Double Weakness of Girls: Discrimination and Sexual Violence in Haiti." *Stanford Journal of International Law* 44 (1), 147.

———. 2009. "What Have Women Got to Do with Peace? A Gender Analysis of the Laws of War and Peacemaking." *Georgetown Journal of Gender and the Law* 10: 37–62. Reprinted in *Law and Outsiders: Norms, Processes, and 'Othering' in the 21st Century*, edited by Cian C. Murphy and Penny Green, 209–232. Oxford: Hart, 2011.

———. 2010. "From Violence against Women to Women's Violence in Haiti." *Columbia Journal of Gender and Law* 19: 1029–1075.

Faedi Duramy, Benedetta. 2011. "Women in the Aftermath of the 2010 Haitian Earthquake." *Emory International Law Review* 25 (3): 1193–1215.

———. 2012. "Gender-Based Violence, Help Seeking, and Criminal Justice Recourse in Haiti." In *Conflict-Related Sexual Violence: International Law, Local Responses*, edited by Tonia St. Germain and Susan Dewey, 103–119. Sterling, VA: Kumarian Press/ Stylus.

Fagan, Jeffrey, and Deanna L. Wilkinson. 1998. "Youth, Violence, and Social Identity in Inner Cities." *Crime and Justice* 24: 105–188.

Fatton, Robert. 2002. *Haiti's Predatory Republic: The Unending Transition to Democracy*. Boulder, CO: Lynne Rienner.

Figueira-McDonough, J. 1989. "Community Structure and Female Delinquency Rates." *Youth & Society* 24: 3–30.

Fort, Sarah. 2006. "HIV in Haiti Is Spread by Violence—and Little Is Done to Prevent the Attacks." International Consortium of Investigative Journalists, November 30. http://www.icij.org/projects/divine-intervention/hiv-haiti-spread-violence -and-little-done-prevent-attacks.

Freedman, B. Estelle. 2002. *No Turning Back: The History of Feminism and the Future of Women*. New York: Ballantine.

Freud, Sigmund. (1905) 1953. "Three Essays on the Theory of Sexuality." In *The Standard Edition of the Complete Psychological Works of Sigmund Freud*, vol. 7, edited and translated by James Strachey. London: Hogarth Press.

———. (1925) 1961. "Some Psychical Consequences of the Anatomical Distinctions between the Sexes." In *The Standard Edition of the Complete Psychological Works of Sigmund Freud*, vol. 19, edited and translated by James Strachey. London: Hogarth Press.

———. (1931) 1961. "Female Sexuality." In *The Standard Edition of the Complete Psychological Works of Sigmund Freud*, vol. 21, edited and translated by James Strachey. London: Hogarth Press.

———. (1933) 1964. "New Introductory Lectures on Psychoanalysis." In *The Standard Edition of the Complete Psychological Works of Sigmund Freud*, vol. 22, edited and translated by James Strachey. London: Hogarth Press.

Gardam, Judith, and Hilary Charlesworth. 2000. "Protection of Women in Armed Conflict." *Human Rights Quarterly* 22: 148–166.

Gibbs, Sara. 1994. "Post-war Social Reconstruction in Mozambique: Re-framing Children's Experience of Trauma and Healing." *Disasters* 18 (3): 268–276.

Gilfus, Mary. 1992. "From Victims to Survivors to Offenders: Women's Routes of Entry and Immersion in Street Crime." *Women and Criminal Justice* 4 (1): 63–90.

Gilligan, Carol. 1982. *In a Different Voice: Psychological Theory and Women's Development*. Cambridge, MA: Harvard University Press.

Haitian Ministry of Social Affairs. 2002. *Les fondements de la pratique de la domesticité des enfants en Haiti* [The foundations of the practice of restavèk in Haiti]. Port-au-Prince: Haitian Ministry of Social Affairs.

Hall, Judith. 1978. "Gender Effects in Decoding Nonverbal Cues." *Psychological Bulletin* 85: 845–857.

Hamilton-Phelan, A. 1994. "The Latest Political Weapon in Haiti: Military Rapes of Women and Girls." *Los Angeles Times*, June 5.

Healy, David. 1995. "The U.S. Occupation of Haiti." In *Haitian Frustrations: Dilemmas for U.S. Policy*, edited by Georges A. Fauriol, 36–45. Washington, DC: Center for Strategic and International Studies.

Heidensohn, Francis. 1985. *Women and Crime*. New York: New York University Press.

Heinl, Debs Robert, Jr., and Nancy Gordon Heinl. 1978. *Written in Blood: The History of Haitian People 1492–1971*. Boston: Houghton Mifflin.

Helland A., Kari Karamé, Anita Kristensen, and Inger Skjelsbæk. 1999. *Women and Armed Conflicts*. A Study for the Norwegian Ministry of Foreign Affairs. Oslo: Norwegian Institute of International Affairs.

Hirschon, Renee. 1984. *Women and Property—Women as Property*. Hampshire, UK: Palgrave Macmillan.

Hobson, Matt. 2005. *Forgotten Casualties of War: Girls in Armed Conflict*. http://resourcecentre.savethechildren.se/sites/default/files/documents/2717.pdf.

Human Rights Watch and the National Coalition for Haitian Refugees. 1994. *Rape in Haiti: A Weapon of Terror*. New York: Human Rights Watch.

Institute for Justice and Democracy in Haiti, MADRE, TransAfrica Forum, University of Minnesota Law School Human Rights Litigation and Advocacy Clinic, and University of Virginia School of Law International Human Rights Law Clinic and Human Rights Program. 2010. *Our Bodies Are Still Trembling:*

Haitian Women's Fight against Rape. July. http://www.madre.org/images/uploads/misc/1283377138_2010.07.26%20-%20HAITI%20GBV%20REPORT%20FINAL.pdf.

Institute Interuniversitaire de Recherche et de Developpment. 2010. *Voices from the Shanties: A Post-earthquake Rapid Assessment of Cité Soleil*. March. Port-au-Prince: Institute Interuniversitaire de Recherche et de Developpment.

International Crisis Group. 2006. *Beyond Victimhood: Women's Peacebuilding in Sudan, Congo, and Uganda*. Africa Report 112. June 28. http://www.crisisgroup.org/en/regions/africa/horn-of-africa/112-beyond-victimhood-womens-peacebuilding-in-sudan-congo-and-uganda.aspx.

International Federation of the Red Cross and Red Crescent Societies. 2007. *Guidelines for the Domestic Facilitation and Regulation of International Disaster Relief and Initial Recovery Assistance*. Geneva, Switzerland: International Federation of the Red Cross and Red Crescent Societies.

Justesen, Michael, and Dorte Verner. 2007. *Factors Impacting Youth Development in Haiti*. World Bank Policy Research Working Paper 4110. January. Washington, DC: World Bank.

Kay Fanm. 2007. *Violence envers les femmes et les filles—Bilan de l'année 2006* [Violence against women and girls—Assessment of 2006]. February. Port-au-Prince: Kay Fanm.

Keairns, Yvonne E. 2002. *The Voices of Girl Child Soldiers*. New York: Quaker United Nations Office.

Kennedy, M., and D. Williams. 1995. *Ending Violence against Women in Haiti: Toward a Democratic Recovery*. Report of HAITIwoman Conference. Cambridge, MA: I, II.

Kolbe, R. Athena, and Royce A. Hutson. 2006. "Human Rights Abuse and Other Criminal Violations in Port-au-Prince, Haiti: A Random Survey of Households." *Lancet* 368: 864–873.

Kolbe, A. R., Muggah, R., Hutson, R. A., James, L., Puccio, M., Trzcinski, E., et al. 2010. *Assessing Needs after the Quake: Preliminary Findings from a Randomized Survey of Port-au-Prince Households*. Ann Arbor: University of Michigan.

Kovats-Bernat, J. Christopher. 2006. *Sleeping Rough in Port-au-Prince*. Gainesville: University Press of Florida.

Lerner, Gerda. 1986. *The Creation of Patriarchy*. Oxford: Oxford University Press.

Littlewood, Roland. 1997. "Military Rape." *Anthropology Today* 13 (2): 7–16.

Lombroso, Cesare, and William Ferraro. 1985. *The Female Offender*. London: T. Fisher Unwin.

Maccoby, E. E., and C. N. Jacklin. 1974. *The Psychology of Sex Differences*. Stanford, CA: Stanford University Press.

MacKinnon, Catharine. 2006. "Genocide's Sexuality." In *Are Women Human? and Other International Dialogues*. Cambridge, MA: Belknap Press.

Magloire, Danièle. 2004. "La violence à l'égard des femmes: Une violation constante des droits de la persone" [Violence against women: A constant violation of human rights]. *Chemins Critiques Revue haïtiano-caribéenne* 5 (2): 66–113.

Manigat, Sabine. 1997. "Haiti: The Popular Sectors and the Crisis in Port-au-Prince." In *The Urban Caribbean: Transition to the New Global Economy*, edited by Alejandro

Portes, Carlos Dore-Cabral, and Patricia Landolt, 87–123. Baltimore: Johns Hopkins University Press.

Maternowska, M. Catherine. 2006. *Reproducing Inequities: Poverty and the Politics of Population in Haiti.* New Brunswick, NJ: Rutgers University Press.

Médecins sans Frontières (MSF). 2010. *Emergency Response after the Haiti Earthquake: Choices, Obstacles, Activities, and Finance.* July. http://www.doctorswithoutborders.org/publications/article.cfm?id=4581.

Merlet, Myriam. 2002. "Between Love, Anger, and Madness: Building Peace in Haiti." In *The Aftermath: Women in Post-Conflict Transformation,* edited by Sheila Meintjes, Anu Pillay, and Meredeth Turshen, 159–171. London: Zed Books.

———. 2010. "Haiti: Women in Conquest of Full and Total Citizenship in an Endless Transition." In *Women's Activism in Latin America and the Caribbean: Engendering Social Justice, Democratizing Citizenship,* edited by Elizabeth Maier and Nathalie Lebon, 127–139. New Brunswick, NJ: Rutgers University Press; Tijuana, Mexico: El Colegio de la Frontera Norte A.C.

Meron, T. 1993. "Rape as a Crime under International Humanitarian Law." *American Journal of International Law* 87: 424–428.

Moitt, Bernard. 2001. *Women and Slavery in the French Antilles 1635–1848.* Bloomington: Indiana University Press.

Ness, Cindy D. 2004. *Why Girls Fight: Female Youth Violence in the Inner City.* New York: New York University Press.

Panos-Caraibes. 2007. "Viol en Haiti: Portraits de filles et de femmes victimes. Témoignages sur le viol en Haiti" [Rape in Haiti: Portraits of girls and women victims. Testimonies on rape in Haiti]. Press release 14. February. http://panoscaribbean.org/wp-content/uploads/documents/dossier_viol_en_haiti_portraits_de_filles_et_de_femmes_victimes.pdf.

Perusse, Roland. 1995. *Haitian Democracy Restored 1991–1995.* Lanham, MD: University Press of America.

Pezzullo, Ralph. 2006. *Plunging into Haiti: Clinton, Aristide, and the Defeat of Diplomacy.* Jackson: University Press of Mississippi.

Pillai, Priya. 2008. "A 'Call to Arms': A Gender-Sensitive Approach to the Plight of Female Child Soldiers in International Law." *Human Rights Brief* 15 (2): 23–27.

Pittaway, Eileen, Linda Bartolomei, and Susan Rees. 2007. "Gendered Dimensions of the 2004 Tsunami and a Potential Social Work Response in Post-Disaster Situations." *International Social Work* 50: 307–319.

Pollak, Otto. 1950. *The Criminality of Women.* Philadelphia: University of Pennsylvania Press.

Porter, Roy. 1986. "Rape—Does It Have a Historical Meaning?" In *Rape: An Historical and Social Enquiry,* edited by Sylvana Tomasell and Ray Porter. Hoboken, NJ: Blackwell.

Puechguirbal, Nadine. 2004. "Involving Women in Peace-Processes: Lessons from Four African Countries." In *Gender and Peace-Building in Africa,* edited by Kari Karamé, 47–68. Oslo: Norwegian Institute of International Affairs.

Puechguirbal, Nadine, Natalie Man, and Wiza Loutis. 2009. "Haiti: The Gendered Pattern of Small-Arms Violence against Women." In *Sexed Pistols: The Gendered Impact of Small Arms and Light Weapons*, edited by Vanessa Farr, Henri Myrttine, and Albrecht Schnabel. New York: United Nations.

Reynolds, Edward. 1985. *Stand the Storm: A History of the Atlantic Slave Trade*. London: Allison & Busby.

Rhodes, Jean, and K. Fischer. 1993. "Spanning the Gender Gap: Gender Differences in Delinquency among Inner-City Adolescents." *Adolescence* 28: 879–889.

Rotberg, Robert I. 1988. "Haiti's Past Mortgages Its Future." *Foreign Affairs* 67 (1): 93–109.

Runtz, Marsha, and John Briere. 1986. "Adolescent 'Acting Out' and Childhood History of Sexual Abuse." *Journal of Interpersonal Violence* 1: 326–334.

Sananes, Gaston. 2007. *Evaluation de la brigade de protection de mineurs* [Assessment of the brigade for the protection of minors]. March. New York: UNICEF.

Sanday Reeves, Peggy. 1990. *Fraternity Gang Rape: Sex, Brotherhood, and Privilege on Campus*. New York: New York University Press.

Schaffner, Laurie. 2006. *Girls in Trouble with the Law*. New Brunswick, NJ: Rutgers University Press.

———. 2007. "Violence against Girls Provokes Girls' Violence: From Private Injury to Public Harm." *Violence against Women* 13 (12): 1229–1248.

Scheper-Hughes, Nancy. 1992. *Death without Weeping: The Violence of Everyday Life in Brazil*. Berkeley: University of California Press.

Seifert, Ruth. 1994. "War and Rape: A Preliminary Analysis." In *Mass Rape: The War against Women in Bosnia-Herzegovina*, edited by Alexandra Stiglmayer; translated by Marion Faber, 54–72. Lincoln: University of Nebraska Press.

Sharlah, Lisa. 1999. "Gender and Genocide in Rwanda: Women as Agents and Objects of Genocide." *Journal of Genocide Research* 1 (3): 387–400.

Sheckleford, Michale. 2006. *Haiti's Dirty Little Secret: The Problem of Child Slavery*. Council on Hemispheric Affairs. September. http://www.coha.org/haiti's -dirty-little-secret-the-problem-of-child-slavery/.

Sikes, Gini. 1998. *8 Ball Chicks: A Year in the Violent World of Girl Gangs*. New York: Anchor Books.

Smith Fawzi, M. C., W. Lambert, J. M. Singler, Y. Tanagho, F. Léandre, P. Nevil, D. Bertrand, D. Claude, M. Loissaint, L. Jeannis, J. S. Mukherjee, S. Goldie, J. J. Salazar, and P. E. Farmer. 2005. "Factors Associated with Forced Sex among Women Accessing Health Services in Rural Haiti: Implications for the Prevention of HIV Infection and Other Sexually Transmitted Diseases." *Social Science & Medicine* 60.

SOFA. 2007. *Rapport bilan IV, cas de violence accueillis et accompagnés dans les centres douvanjou de la SOFA de juillet à decembre 2006* [Assessment report IV, cases of violence received and accompanied by the SOFA centers from July to December 2006]. January. Port-au-Prince: SOFA.

———. 2010. *Rapport bilan 10, cas de violences accueillis et accompagnes dans les 21 centres douvanjou de la SOFA de janvier a juin 2010* [Assessment report 10, cases of violence received and accompanied by the SOFA centers from January to June 2010]. November. Port-au-Prince: SOFA.

Sommerfelt, Tone. 2002. *Child Domestic Labour in Haiti—Characteristics, Contexts, and Organization of Children's Residence, Relocation, and Work.* Report to UNICEF, ILO, Save the Children UK, and Save the Children Canada. May. Oslo: Fafo Institute for Applied International Studies.

St. Fleur, Jean Max. 2006. "Un certificat médical gratuit aux victimes d'agressions sexuelles" [Free medical certificate for victims of sexual assaults]. *Le Nouvelliste* (Port-au-Prince), November 24.

Steffensmeier, Darrell, and E. Allan. 1991. "Gender, Age, and Crime." In *Criminology: A Contemporary Hand-Book*, edited by J. F. Sheley, 67–93. Belmont, CA: Wadsworth.

Table de Concertation Nationale sur les Violences Faites aux Femmes. 2005a. *Plan national de lutte contre les violences faites aux femmes: Prevention, prise en charge et accompagnement des victimes de violences specifiques faites aux femmes, 2006–2011* [National plan to fight against violence against women: Prevention and care and accompaniment of victims of specific forms of violence against women, 2006–2011]. November. Port-au-Prince: Table de Concertation Nationale sur les Violences Faites aux Femmes.

———. 2005b. *Rapport de Commission de Collecte des Données* [Report of the Commission for the Collection of Data]. November. Port-au-Prince: Table de Concertation Nationale sur les Violences Faites aux Femmes.

Thomas, Dorothy Q., and Michele E. Beasley. 1993. "Domestic Violence as a Human Rights Issue." *Human Rights Quarterly* 15 (1): 36–62.

Tickner, Ann. 1992. *Gender in International Relations: Feminist Perspectives on Achieving Global Security.* New York: Columbia University Press.

Tiger, Lionel. 1969. *Men in Groups.* New York: Random House.

Tiger, Lionel, and Robin Fox. 1970. *The Imperial Animal.* New York: Holt, Rinehart and Winston.

United Nations. 1995. *The Fourth World Conference on Women: Action for Equality, Development, and Peace, Beijing Declaration and Platform for Action.* U.N. GAOR, U.N. Doc. A/CONF.177/20.

———. 2003. *The Role of Men and Boys in Achieving Gender Equality: Report of the Expert Group Meeting, Brasilia, Brazil, October 2003.* http://www.un.org/womenwatch/daw/egm/men-boys2003/reports/Finalreport.PDF.

———. 2006. *In-Depth Study on All Forms of Violence against Women: Report of the Secretary-General.* July 6. http://daccess-dds-ny.un.org/doc/UNDOC/GEN/N06/419/74/PDF/N0641974.pdf?OpenElement.

United Nations Department of Peacekeeping Operations. 2004. *Gender Resource Package for Peacekeeping Operations Produced by Peacekeeping Best Practice Unit.* New York: United Nations.

United Nations Economic and Social Council. 2000. *Integration of the Human Rights of Women and the Gender Perspective: Violence against Women, Report of the United Nations Special Rapporteur on Violence against Women on the Mission to Haiti.* E/CN4./2000/68/Add. 3. January 27. http://www.unhchr.ch/Huridocda/Huridoca.nsf/0/1961657f6bc303f9802568ba004b4b3b?Opendocument.

United Nations Economic and Social Council, Commission on Human Rights. 2006. *Integration of the Human Rights of Women and the Gender Perspective: Violence against Women. The Due Diligence Standard as a Tool for the Elimination of Violence against Women.* Report of the Special Rapporteur on Violence against Women, Its Causes and Consequences, Yakin Ertürk. E/CN.4/2006/61, January 20. http://www.refworld.org/pdfid/45377afb0.pdf.

United Nations General Assembly. 2006. *Report of the Special Representative of the Secretary-General for Children and Armed Conflict.* U.N. DOC No. A/61/275, August 17. http://www.essex.ac.uk/armedcon/story_id/000670.pdf.

———. 2007. *Report of the Special Representative of the Secretary-General for Children and Armed Conflict.* U.N. DOC No. A/62/228, August 13. http://www.refworld.org/docid/47316f602.html.

United Nations General Assembly/Security Council. 2005. *Children and Armed Conflict: Report of the Secretary-General.* A/61/529-S/2006/826. October 26. http://www.securitycouncilreport.org/atf/cf/%7B65BFCF9B-6D27-4E9C-8CD3-CF6E4FF96FF9%7D/CAC%20S2006%20826.pdf.

———. 2006. *Children and Armed Conflict: Report of the Secretary-General.* A/61/529-S/2006/826. October 26. http://www.securitycouncilreport.org/atf/cf/%7B65BFCF9B-6D27-4E9C-8CD3-CF6E4FF96FF9%7D/CAC%20S2006%20826.pdf.

United Nations High Commissioner for Refugees. 2003. *Sexual and Gender-Based Violence against Refugees, Returnees, and Internally Displaced Persons: Guidelines for Prevention and Response.* May. http://www.refworld.org/docid/3edcd0661.html.

United Nations International Children's Emergency Fund (UNICEF). 2006. *Child Alert: Haiti.* March. http://www.unicef.org/childalert/haiti/content/Child%20Alert%20Haiti%20(En).pdf.

———. 2007. *The Paris Principles: Principles and Guidelines on Children Associated with Armed Forces or Armed Groups.* February. http://www.refworld.org/docid/465198442.html.

United Nations Office for the Coordination of Humanitarian Affairs (OCHA). 1998. *Guiding Principles on Internal Displacement.* http://reliefweb.int/sites/reliefweb.int/files/resources/AB752ABEA5C1EFFCC1256C33002A8510-idp.html.

———. 2000. *The Handbook for Applying the Guiding Principles on Internal Displacement.* http://www.refworld.org/docid/3d52a6432.html.

United Nations Population Fund (UNFPA). 1999. *Violence against Girls and Women: A Public Health Priority.* New York: United Nations Population Fund.

United Nations Security Council. 2009. *Report of the Security Council Mission to Haiti (11 to 14 March 2009).* S/2009/175. April 3. http://daccess-dds-ny.un.org/doc/UNDOC/GEN/N09/290/34/PDF/N0929034.pdf?OpenElement.

———. 2010a. *Report of the Secretary-General on the United Nations Stabilization Mission in Haiti.* S/2010/200. February 22. http://www.un.org/en/ga/search/view_doc.asp?symbol=S/2010/200.

———. 2010b. *Report of the Secretary-General on the United Nations Stabilization Mission in Haiti.* S/2010/446, September 1. http://www.un.org/en/ga/search/view_doc.asp?symbol=S/2010/446.

United Nations Stabilization Mission in Haiti (MINUSTAH), Human Rights Section. 2010. *IDP Camp Joint Security Assessment (JSA) Report*. Port-au-Prince: United Nations Stabilization Mission in Haiti.

United Nations Stabilization Mission in Haiti (MINUSTAH) and United Nations Development Programme in Haiti (UNDP). 2006. *The Situation of Women in the Context of Armed Violence in Haiti*. June. New York: United Nations.

United States Agency for International Development (USAID). 2010. *USAID's Approach to Shelter in Post-earthquake Haiti: Providing Security, Dignity, and Work*. May 26. http://pdf.usaid.gov/pdf_docs/PDACP673.pdf.

Wesely, Jennifer K. 2006. "Considering the Context of Women's Violence—Gender, Lived Experiences, and Cumulative Victimization." *Violence against Women* 1 (4): 303–328.

West, Harry G. 2000. "Girls with Guns: Narrating the Experience of War of FRELIMO's 'Female Detachment.'" *Anthropological Quarterly* 73 (4): 180–194. http://www.jstor.org/stable/3318250.

Wolfe, Leslie, and Jennifer Tucker. 1998. *Report of the Summit on Girls and Violence*. Washington, DC: Center for Women Policy Studies.

World Bank. 2006a. *Haiti: Enhanced Heavily Indebted Poor Countries (HIPC) Initiative: Preliminary Document*. Report 36917. Washington, DC: World Bank. http://documents.worldbank.org/curated/en/2006/08/7067353/haiti-enhanced-heavily-indebted-poor-countries-hipc-initiative-preliminary-document.

———. 2006b. *Social Resilience and State Fragility in Haiti*. Washington, DC: World Bank. https://openknowledge.worldbank.org/handle/10986/6836.

World Health Organization (WHO). 2005. *Multi-country Study on Women's Health and Domestic Violence against Women*. Geneva: World Health Organization.

INDEX

ABOUT THE AUTHOR

BENEDETTA FAEDI DURAMY is an associate professor of law at Golden Gate University School of Law in San Francisco, where she teaches international human rights, gender and children's issues in international law, international humanitarian law, and property. She is the author of several book chapters and articles on human rights, gender issues, and children's rights. She obtained her doctoral degree from Stanford Law School, Stanford University, where she was the recipient of numerous awards for her extensive research and scholarship on gender-based violence, with a special focus on Haiti.

Review Notes

Many different sources cited for further reading and lots of statistical evidence

Stark contrast of cold + striking statistics w/ personal narratives makes the book an engaging and captivating read, and the reader feels immense empathy for the women telling their stories.

This work comes from the unique perspective of _why_ women participate in violence rather than to what degree. First research of its kind in Haiti; Brings statistic and numeric evidence of strong correlations and trends between being victimized and carrying out violence for revenge or control

Candid tone of interviewees presents horrors like facts of life and successfully puts into context the related feelings + actions.

CPSIA information can be obtained at www.ICGtesting.com
Printed in the USA
BVOW04s1747240314

348596BV00002B/2/P

9 780813 563145